STEWARDSHIP GOD'S WAY

GOOD STEWARDSHIP FOR THE GOOD SHEPHERD

KENDALL DAVIS

Reliquia
PUBLISHING
CHERISHING STORIES FOR A LIFETIME

Unless otherwise noted, all scripture quotations are from the World English Bible (WEB) 2020. All texts of the WEB are dedicated to the public domain. The World English Bible is an updated revision of the American Standard Version, published in 1901. Quotations marked KJV are from the King James Version, Public domain. Scriptures marked NIV are from the New International Version 2011

This book does not endorse any specific financial products, such as particular stocks, commodities, or money market account brands. The content is based on the standards of stewardship and money management found in the Bible. However, biblical principles apply to all, as they are directed towards believers living in covenant with God, who loves them and desires their best outcomes. The author does not vouch for the complete content of any books or sites quoted, but only for the material found in the direct quote.

Also, by Kendall Davis

Blessed on Purpose
A Daily Devotional on Christian Living

In His Image Volume I
A Daily Devotional for Spiritual Transformation

200 Tips for a Successful Marriage

I thank my wife and children for their support, but I dedicate this book to you, the reader. Yes, I'm talking about you, the one who shows an interest in handling Stewardship God's Way. I commend you for your commitment to faithfulness and for taking steps towards achieving financial security. If no one has ever dedicated a book to you before, you can place your name here right now. This book is for and about you.

This Book is Dedicated to: _____

Continue to be faithful and fantastic.

CONTENTS

PREFACE

If you've had an idea or project that you've picked up and set back down several times, something you couldn't complete but couldn't leave alone, you will understand that this book is my story of that. It has been written, taught in churches, and spoken about, only to be shelved for years, then to find itself revisited, revised, and resurrected. I am here to tell everyone with a dream, vision, or imagination that you will **REAP (Recover Every Asset Planted)** fruit from your efforts if you keep pressing forward. The church has become expert at teaching sowing, but few teach you how to reap, and more importantly, they don't teach you how to maintain what you have gained. If we are going to learn, it should be from start to completion.

As citizens of the kingdom of heaven and children of God, we are responsible for properly handling the **TEST (Things, Events, Situations & Thoughts)** we have. That's what stewardship responsibility is all about. Those who want to live an abundant life must operate with a mindset that receives and embraces the blessings and promises Christ gives. People who wait around for things to happen are often unprepared when they do. Opportunity comes only to slip through their fingers. This book enhances our awareness and discipline, enabling us to operate with greater financial stability, responsibility, and freedom.

Stewardship God's Way is a standalone book that offers valuable wisdom on biblical stewardship. However, there is an application guidebook and videos that provide additional materials to enhance the concepts discussed throughout the book. Scan the QR codes found in each chapter to link to the video. The goal is to provide instruction through reading and interactive videos to motivate the learner, along with a guidebook to help initiate the application of these principles in practice. Those familiar with my writing style will notice that the chapter titles are also titles of other works. Each is a title of a book on stewardship that you can read, and there are acronyms to boot. I hope you enjoy reflecting on everything written here.

CHAPTER ONE

KINGDOM STEWARDSHIP

· · · · · · · · · · · ·

1 CORINTHIANS 4:2

Here, moreover, it is required of stewards
that they be found faithful.

W hen I was young, people would tell me to hide my money under the mattress. Banks were not always easily accessible, especially in impoverished neighborhoods, and because there was less regulation, some people didn't trust their practices. There were stories of people who had hidden money for so long that others discovered small fortunes in their homes after they passed away. This practice of hiding money in the house was so widespread that everyone suspected they had a secretly rich aunt or uncle who had hoarded but never spent their money. Hoarding is what some believe to be a form of stewardship. They hid money away and didn't trust banks or the stock market in case of a nationwide economic crisis. The truth is, most of us don't have a secret, rich relative we've never met who will leave us their entire estate. In fact, most people would likely squander what they have if someone were to leave them a lump sum, because they do not understand the principles of stewardship or how money works.

THE KING'S STEWARD

That brings us to the question of what a steward is. Is it simply a high position in a king's court? We often don't think in line with what it means to be a steward. Synonyms such as administrator, porter, or curator often come to mind. The biblical term for steward means "Man over the House." They are a chosen person given responsibility within their ability to manage the affairs, household, or properties according to the desires of the one they serve. It is a relationship of trust and accountability. The **STEWARD (Servant Tasks Engages Wealth And Responsible Duty)** is the house manager who utilizes the resources God has given to glorify Him and bless His kingdom. As citizens of the Kingdom of God, we have been given a stewardship over all that our Lord has entrusted to us. God requires faithfulness from all of His servants. There are certain things that we must know to be good stewards.

GOD OWNS EVERYTHING

People incorrectly say that when the Lord created Adam, He relinquished control over the earth to man. Then, when man sinned, Satan wrested that control from humankind. Nothing can be further from the truth. God did not relinquish control; He gave man the authority he needed to be a steward over all the earth. Satan owns nothing. He was a bad steward who got fired from his job and now hangs around as a disgruntled former employee, giving bad reviews and trying to tear down the place he wishes he still worked at. Two bible verses incorrectly mislead some to believe that this world belongs to Satan. The first is 2 Corinthians 4:4, where the bible calls Satan "the god of this world". The second is Matthew 4:8-9, where Satan offers the kingdoms of the world to Jesus if He would only bow down to him.

At first glance, the devil may appear to be in control of the world, but he is not. What Satan controls is the systems of manipulation by which a fallen world operates. His control is the power to manipulate and affect the behavior of those who listen to him and buy into his system. He does this through tempting thoughts that wrestle against the Spirit of truth, by implanting ideas that promote selfish gain by exploiting others, and by making suggestions that resist repentance and the formation of a good heart. His **TIS (Thoughts, Ideas, Suggestions)** are his only weapons since Jesus disarmed the spiritual rulers and authorities, making a public spectacle of them through His triumph on the cross (Colossians 2:15). Satan only controls those whom he has blinded to the truth. The bible says:

> *1 Chronicles 29:11 Yours, Yahweh, is the greatness, the power, the glory, the victory, and the majesty! For all that is in the heavens and in the earth is yours. Yours is the kingdom, Yahweh, and you are exalted as head above all.*

The Hebrew word "Ro'sh" is used here to indicate that God is the head above all, signifying firstness, chief, or primacy, which emphasizes the supremacy of God's authority. In a sense, it means God is on top. For those who know what it's like at the bottom, reaching for the top is a way of life. Not only is God above all things, but He is on top of all things in your life. Shake the tree too hard, and you will eventually see that God is there. He is both the root and the fruit of the tree that will build your future.

> *Psalms 24:1 The earth is Yahweh's, with its fullness; the world, and those who dwell in it.*

This verse speaks of the Sphere of God's authority. Not only does the earth belong to the Lord, but everything it contains. God's ownership isn't limited to things like mountains and rivers, but all of nature, including us. According to Genesis, the earth was formless and void, and God spent the first three days of creation giving the world form and the next three days filling the things formed during the first three days. God forms day and night on the first day, then fills it with the sun, moon, and stars on the fourth day. He formed the seas and sky on the second day and filled them with fish and birds on the fifth day. While the land formed on the third day of creation became filled with vegetation, animal life appeared on the sixth day. The earth, being the Lord's property, speaks to His creation of it. The fullness refers to everything He made in the second set of three days. Initially, everything in those days submitted to God, and humanity became God's stewards over all He had made.

> *Leviticus 25:23 The land shall not be sold in perpetuity, for the land is mine; for you are strangers and live as foreigners with me.*

God told the Israelites that they were not to sell the land He had given them outright, because it belonged to Him, and they were only on a lease agreement. The terms of the lease were to be faithful to Him. As long as they made the Lord their God, He would make them His people. Yet they are to remember that they are still aliens and tenants living on what belonged to Him. The significance of God's authority is stated in Isaiah 45:18, which says that God did not create the earth to remain void, like some dead planet, but made it for the habitation of life. God's authority is not purposeless or blind; it has significance in placing people in a state of favor. They were not to rid themselves of the land God gave, but to work on it. During times of hardship, He may allow the land to be leased so that others can work it and bring the profit back to you, yet your stewardship does not permit abandoning responsibility.

Haggai 2:8 "The silver is mine and the gold is mine,' declares the Lord Almighty

---

Reading this verse in isolation would cause you to think that it is talking about the finances of the believer, but it's not. When the Israelites, who were familiar with the former temple, saw the new temple, they thought it was small in comparison to it. However, God assured them that the new glory would outshine the old glory and that if the Spirit of God remained among them, He would shake heaven, earth, and the nations of the world, who would bring their silver and gold in. The sufficiency of God's authority is in His ability to cause increase to the faithful. Not only does He care for you, He will take care of you. More than anything else, we need God's Spirit with us, giving us warning and direction as we go forth in this world.

WHY THE HOARDING?

Hoarding comes from fear and selfishness. People stored money at home out of fear. In case you don't remember what led to the Great Depression, on Black Thursday, October 24, 1929, the US stock market crashed, sending investors into a state of panic. The crash contributed significantly to the eventual collapse of the banking system and led to an unemployment rate that skyrocketed to 24.9%. Due to all the years of hardship and recovery, you can understand why post-depression era adults hid their money under mattresses. But what importance is this today? We live in an era in which regulations have reduced the risk of loss of savings by federally insuring deposits up to a certain amount. Although the stock market remains risky, there are safeguards in place to prevent a free fall. These safety circuit breakers halt trading, allowing investors to understand what is happening in the market before withdrawing or re-entering. Why does this matter? Well, because Stewardship is responsibility. You must know your situation and opportunities to secure the best advantage for your family and goals.

EVERYTHING WE HAVE COMES FROM GOD

As stewards, we are not owners, but instead managers of everything that comes from God. The Lord gives us possessions and wants us to use wisdom in how to spend, save, or care for what He has given us. A steward uses the provision given to him to care for his self, his family, all those who are under his authority, and most importantly, the business of his Lord.

POWER TO GET WEALTH

Faithfulness rather than wealth generation is the primary goal of stewardship. However, covenant wealth may occur if one follows the ways God has laid out for them. What is covenant wealth? Deuteronomy 8:18 reads, *"But you shall remember Yahweh your God, for it is he who gives you power to get wealth, that he may establish his covenant which he swore to your fathers, as it is today."* Covenant wealth is an endowment of favor and wisdom that, when combined with sound financial strategies and effective partnerships, contributes to growth and increase. Please take into account that the Jewish people are only 0.2% of the world's population, but account for 20% of its billionaires. This anomaly is one hundred times what we expect to see. We will discuss the wisdom, professionalism, patience, and generosity it takes to do this in later chapters, but the hundredfold blessing isn't an accident; it's a strategy. Not only do they give, but they also help each other. If one opens a business, they will have five companies that will choose them as a vendor to support them financially until they get established. Most people consider their product or service first when starting a business; however, the Jewish community practices building relationships with companies as they develop the business or service, rather than approaching them after the finished product is ready. To the Jewish people, wealth is about spiritual growth and community responsibility just as much as it is about security.

THE ABILITY TO RECEIVE

The book of Ecclesiastes may seem cynical, but it is a practical way to help people appreciate the life they have. Ecclesiastes 5:19 reads, *"Every man also to whom God has given riches and wealth, and has given him power to eat of it, and to take his portion, and to rejoice in his labor—this is the gift of God."* Life isn't fair, so we must take the time to appreciate the beauty around us as we go along, or we will miss the beautiful gardens while focusing on the thorns. If money becomes your everything, and you lose it, you will have nothing. However, losing money isn't the same as losing everything. Our life is about more than what we have. Charles Spurgeon put it this way, "It is not how much we have, but how much we enjoy, that makes happiness." If you take a business away from an entrepreneur, they will still have the knowledge and skill to build another one. The only things that stop us from moving forward are the fear of failure and a lack of confidence.

A GENEROUS HEART

I know I said we would talk about generosity in later chapters, but let's get a jump-start now, at least on one aspect of it. David spent years preparing for the transition of the kingdom to his son Solomon, who was to build the temple. Not only did he provide the necessary finances, but he also spent time organizing the priestly factions into well-structured functions, each with its specific responsibilities. All this for something he would not build. David asks in 1 Chronicles 29:14, *"But who am I, and what is my people, that we should be able to offer so willingly as this? For all things come from you, and we have given you of your own.*" David never pursued wealth; he pursued God, and he used his wealth to become a benefactor. There were things he could not do on his own, but he had a heart to contribute to the work of others. Generosity contributes to helping others where you can't. You may not be able to build the schools, dig the wells, or even reach many through the gospel or discipleship, but you can help others with the passion to do so by providing your support. Ronald Reagan said, "We can accomplish anything as long as no one cares who gets the credit." We can do it if our **HEARTS (Hearing Ears Always Respond To Sensitivity)** are in the right place. Solomon would receive the recognition, but David would have the reward of sponsoring the project. His generous heart allowed them both to accomplish their dream.

DEDICATION TO BRING GOD GLORY

> Romans 11:36 *For of him and through him and to him are all things. To him be the glory for ever! Amen.*

Not everyone wants to be wealthy. We each set our own goals. For some, budgeting to get out of debt and saving a little nest egg for retirement is enough. We determine our income by the type of business or vocation we pursue. Having a side hustle and gaining passive income through investments is great. However, stewardship is ultimately about making the most of what you have. Working for the satisfaction of helping others in a lower-paying job brings us a different kind of wealth, called joy. A faithful servant of God lives their life for God's glory, not their own. This is the heart of a faithful steward. Because they are people of God, they accomplish their deeds through cooperation with His guidance, and everything is to the Lord. Doing right is its own reward, and God rewards us greatly when we continue to do right.

MONEY IS A TOOL, GOD IS A MASTER

> Malachi 1:6 *"A son honors his father, and a servant his master. If I am a father, then where is my honor? And if I am a master, where is the respect due me?" says Yahweh of Armies to you priests who despise my name. "You say, 'How have we despised your name?'"*

We have a dual relationship as children and as servants. Better put, we are God's children faithfully working for the betterment of our whole household. Our goal is to make the household whole, ensuring that we lack nothing good. God intends His provision to serve a purpose, not just for pleasure. While money has its place in the world, it should not become a Christian's primary **GOAL (Getting Opportunities And Learning)**. Money is to be used purposefully and not abused personally. Luke 16:13 says, *"No servant can serve two masters, for either he will hate the one and love the other; or else he will hold to one and despise the other. You aren't able to serve God and Mammon."* Mammon is more than just money; it encompasses material wealth and the entities that promise it. These entities can be bosses, wealth managers, investors, or influencers who make great promises but often fail to deliver. When they do deliver, there is often a hint of shrewdness, exploitation, or manipulation that we would not wish to be associated with. Mammon is likely derived from the Hebrew contraction Mihamon, with Mi, meaning "from," and hāmōn, meaning "accumulation. So, mammon isn't just money; it includes the heart's desire to pursue gain, which influences our choices.

Instead of saying that you cannot serve God and mammon, Jesus could have said that you can't serve God and the devil. However, he knew how attractive the devil can be when he disguises himself as influence and opportunity. When we have to choose between God and the devil, we choose God, but when we have to choose between God and money, many believers struggle. Satan fights indirectly by putting temptations before us, knowing that choosing them is a rejection of God's grace. His fight is to rob us of the grace that will transform our lives. So, why not tempt us with something delicious, delightful, and desirable just as He did with Eve in Genesis 3:6 which says, *"When the woman saw that the tree was good for food, and that it was a delight to the eyes, and that the tree was to be desired to make one wise, she took some of its fruit, and ate. Then she gave some to her husband with her, and he ate it, too."* John calls these the lust for the flesh, lust of the eyes, and pride of life in 1 John 2:16. These are the temptations the world continually lays before us that cause believers to choose them over God's grace.

People often point out that Jesus spoke frequently about money. Eleven out of 39 parables spoke of money, or even that one out of every seven verses Jesus spoke, alluded to money. He actually spoke more about food, but that's the trouble with statistics. They can state the facts and miss the point simultaneously. When Jesus spoke of money, money was never the point He was making. He was speaking of the kingdom, righteousness, forgiveness, and dedicated service. He uses things like money, food, drink, and desires to contrast the temptations that Satan and the world use to rob us of grace. That's where the rubber meets the road. Who will you follow, God or your own desires? Following God leads to salvation; following your own desires leads to the broad road of destruction.

Mammon is the influencer Satan attempted to use when he spoke to Jesus, saying, 'All these I will give to you if you just bow down' (Matthew 4:9). Satan would have us pursue money instead of God, However the bible says: *"But seek first God's Kingdom and his righteousness; and all these things will be given to you as well" (Matthew 6:33).* The things that we want and worry about God promises to give through seeking Him. Did you notice how similar the concepts in these two verses are? Satan says to bow to him, and he will give you what you want. Jesus says to seek God's kingdom and righteousness, and God will give you everything you need. Both concepts involve receiving provision by seeking an individual. However, Satan offers us a temporary thing to steal away the permanent things God wants to give us. It's not just that we won't serve two masters; some of us have tried and failed to do so. It's that we can't serve two masters. Eventually, priorities will conflict, and one will have to take precedence over the others. Will we stick to our God-first convictions, or will we just let this one slip, get us closer to our goals, and ask God to forgive us later? Spiritual Death happens one compromise at a time.

KEEPING GOD AS MASTER

Jehovah our God is Lord over all. Being Lord means He is the only one to whom we are to surrender our lives. 1 Corinthians 6:12 reads, *"All things are lawful for me, but not all things are expedient. All things are lawful for me, but I will not be brought under the power of anything."* The Bible gives several principles that, if followed, will help keep us from being lured into the money trap.

THE MONEY TRAP

> *Luke 12:15 He said to them, "Beware! Keep yourselves from covetousness, for a man's life doesn't consist of the abundance of the things which he possesses."*

Loving money is a weapon the enemy uses to pull us down. A 1967 movie classic, entitled "The Money Trap," starring Glenn Ford and Rita Hayworth, highlighted the perils of chasing money. Without giving away too many spoilers, it shows how Mammon's appeal to change one's lifestyle lures the cast one by one into destruction. You may wonder, what is the money trap? It's our greed. **GREED (Getting Rich Eposes Excessive Desire)** is a sly fox. It is a well from which men drink and are never satisfied. It derives from selfish desires and eventually consumes one's thoughts, taking over their heart. Ecclesiastes 5:10 says, *"He who loves silver shall not be satisfied with silver, nor he who loves abundance, with increase. This also is vanity."* Instead of becoming more assured, greed is a lack of security that feeds on envy and impatience, leading to ruined lives. Here are a few things to consider about the dangers of being overly influenced by wealth.

THE INFLUENCE OF WEALTH MAY ULTIMATELY END IN MISERY.

1 Timothy 6:9-10 But those who are determined to be rich fall into a temptation, a snare, and many foolish and harmful lusts, such as drown men in ruin and destruction. For the love of money is a root of all kinds of evil. Some have been led astray from the faith in their greed, and have pierced themselves through with many sorrows.

Wealth gives an illusion of contentment, joy, and a trouble-free life. However, when we examine many successful people, we find that they worry about who loves them for who they are and who is out for their **MONEY (Momentarily Owned Not Eternally Yours)**. The illusion has us dwelling on dreams and forgetting to live rightly. It leads to insecurity and controlling relationships. Their well-being is often subjective, based on what they have, rather than on emotionally stable relationships that foster their esteem and self-worth. Being wealthy doesn't stop anxiety, depression, or help with grief. Wealth may provide a temporary retreat, but too often people retreat so deeply into it that they fail to address their emotional issues and problems.

On the other hand, others have sacrificed the most essential things in their lives to chase after wealth. They have added to their stress and caused emotional damage to loved ones and their own souls. Temptations to compromise and leave behind biblical principles of stewardship arise as God removes the hedge of protection that once surrounded them. When you cut corners, you cut people and remove your hedge. The hedge is a protective barrier set around the believer as they abide by God's instructions. Hedges are grown, and some attacks will get through until you are fully covered, like Job after all his struggles.

SEEKING MONEY SHOWS A LACK OF SELF-RESTRAINT.

> *Proverbs 23:4-5 Don't weary yourself to be rich. In your wisdom, show restraint. Why do you set your eyes on that which is not? For it certainly sprouts wings like an eagle and flies in the sky.*

Restraint is not stagnant; instead, it is a deliberate action or inaction reflecting God-given wisdom. It enables us to make the right moves at the correct times and avoid panicking over finances. The steward's life may be hectic, but they must learn to operate with a calm spirit. The more rushed you may feel, the further behind you will get. One noticeable characteristic regarding wisdom is that everyone we consider wise is very patient. Without **WISDOM (Wise Insight Shifts, Discernment Opening Minds),** you will find yourself responding to fear and trends without acting financially responsibly. Wearing yourself out for riches that may leave faster than you can earn them is foolish.

SEEKING MONEY SHOWS A LACK OF PURPOSE AND VISION.

Ecclesiastes 5:10-11 He who loves silver shall not be satisfied with silver, nor he who loves abundance, with increase. This also is vanity. When goods increase, those who eat them are increased; and what advantage is there to its owner, except to feast on them with his eyes?

Money is a good servant but a bad master. It's better to either work for a purpose or work with a purpose. The best companies typically began with a clear purpose of something they wanted to achieve or create. Perhaps we are all aware that Amazon began as an online book broker with the goal of becoming a multiproduct platform, now recognized as the "everything store." But several small businesses also started with a purpose. Someone may have wanted to make something more convenient or worked for a company and thought they could do a better job for customers with a business model they developed. Even if the business did not achieve great success, they could still be satisfied with what they accomplished. Wealth generation became the byproduct of accomplishing that purpose.

Similarly, working with a sense of purpose involves accomplishing the same satisfying goals. You may not have created the business model, but as a steward, God is your employer. It's always better to do the work you love, but even working in a field you once liked can become tedious. Not everyone has the opportunity to work in a location of their choice. Some settle for what pays the bills and must find purpose in serving God in the workplace. Working with a sense that you are there for a purpose increases overall job satisfaction and reduces workplace stress.

THE 10 COMMANDMENTS OF STEWARDSHIP FROM DEUTERONOMY 26

• • • • •

1. You Shall Acquire Property Establishing Wealth For Generations (V.1)

2. You Shall Produce Something That You Can Teach Family Members To Replicate (V.2)

3. You Shall Be Faithful God And Establish God As Your Foundation (V.3)

4. You Shall Remind Yourself Where You Came From And Speak Positively Of Where You Are Going (V.5-9)

5. You Shall Work Hard And Smart Even When You Don't Feel Like It (V.6)

6. You Shall Maintain A Giving Heart (V.10)

7. You Shall Live As If All Your Finances Are Assigned For A Specific Purpose (V.13)

8. You Shall Have A Plan And Stick To It (V.14)

9. You Shall Do The Right Thing, Not The Easy Thing (V.16)

10. You Shall Encourage Yourself And Declare God's Faithfulness (V.17-19)

Scan for video on: Your Spiritual Net Worth

CHAPTER TWO

THE LEGACY JOURNEY

· · · · · · · · · · · ·

ECCLESIASTES 11:6

In the morning sow your seed, and in the evening don't withhold your hand; for you don't know which will prosper, whether this or that, or whether they both will be equally good.

The concept that those who work for others should also work for themselves is a biblical principle. In biblical times, people worked from sunrise to sunset, six days a week, and took a Sabbath day each week to rest, renew their faith, restore their strength, and refresh their minds. The day doesn't end with your eight hours of work. While others are hoping in front of the TV, on the phone, or on social media, take some time to work for yourself by starting a side hustle to bolster your finances and build greater financial security.

The bible contains around 2,000 verses on money, but there are only a few ways to earn money legally and morally, referred to as *PIES (Products, Investments, Eligibilities, Services)* of earning. The laws of countries vary, and the steward of God must remember that not everything legal is moral, and some moral things are not legal. The cryptocurrency market is booming, offering the potential to earn significant money, but it has also seen several rug pulls that have left investors at a loss. A rug pull occurs when individuals who promoted the product steal the funds, a form of fraud known as a hard pull. A soft pull is different and occurs when promoters either sell off their shares or abandon the project, leaving investors with devalued tokens, which is legal but immoral. Assisting with services for those in your nation illegally may be moral, and even the government sometimes bends the rules and helps people who are not their legally because it is a moral thing to do. However, their suspension of the law doesn't change the law. It may be moral to put money in someone's parking meter that has expired right as you see the meter maid approaching, but that doesn't make it quite legal in most places. Some view it as not being helpful to the stewardship of the one parking because you are taking their responsibility and hindering potential growth that could occur when the pain of the ticket causes them to make better future decisions. With that said, let's review the PIES of earning.

PRODUCTS:

Selling **PRODUCTS** *(Produce, Rewards, Organics, Data, Used, Commodities, Textiles, Safeguards)* means there is something that you have produced, processed, provided, put together, or purchased at a lower price that you can sell at a higher price. Produce refers to the fruits and vegetables that grow from the ground, which we eat and purchase at markets. Rewards are rebates that drive customer loyalty towards the continued use of specific goods and services, benefiting both the buyer and the seller. Organics are retail goods, including meat, minerals, and certain medicines, that affect our bodies. Data products encompass internet services, computer programs, social media platforms, and live streaming services. We should never forget that used cars, furniture, and other goods we have can earn back a small percentage of what we initially spent on them. Commodities are raw materials that others use to finish or manufacture their product. Textiles are filaments and fibers that are woven into fabrics, providing our **LUCKY (Linen, Upholstery, Clothing, Knick-knacks, Yarn)** goods. Safeguards refer to warranties, guarantees, and insurance products purchased for after the **FACT (Failure, Accident, Calamity, Tragedy)** occurrences.

INVESTMENTS:

Investing involves using your resources to grow another person's business, service, or product in exchange for a percentage of the expected revenues. It is placing what you have in the hands of another. Risk is a factor in all investments. The simplest investment is a no-risk federally insured savings account or certificate of deposit, where you place your money for a short term. The gains are at or below the federal interest rate, while the better accounts exceed inflation. Financial plans, stock shares, money market accounts, commercial ventures, and properties are other types of investments that are usually long-term and range from low- to high-risk. There is a saying that goes, "The higher the risk, the higher the reward, but also the greater the potential that you may lose your investment".

ELIGIBILITIES:

Eligibilities are not considered earnings by some, as they are things that you qualify for and apply for. Their funding comes from government taxes, private donations, and philanthropic individuals. Eligibility is enabled by government assistance for the individual, such as welfare, to assist financially challenged individuals who meet the LED (Low-Income, Elderly, Disabled) requirements. These government-designed programs were to help those who cannot help themselves until they get back on their feet.

As stewards, we are to be resourceful, and it may require some to apply for federal services for a period, but it should not be our end goal. The time we use should be fruitful. Another type of eligibility is educational scholarships and grants that reduce the need for student loan debt, enabling us to become better equipped to be productive members of society. Unemployment is a government-run eligibility insurance that you have paid into. It replaces a portion of your income and compensates you for prior contributions when you lose your job. In a sense, our income tax return also serves as an eligibility requirement for certain tax breaks that enable us to earn more money. Lastly, eligibility includes assistance for organizations receiving grants to foster services and development deemed necessary by the government and other entities. These programs are to fund social initiatives, but companies and businesses can also benefit from them. During the COVID-19 pandemic, many individuals and companies in the USA applied for the government Paycheck Protection Program, which provided employers with funds to pay their employees, often without repayment.

SERVICES:

Selling services involves leveraging your abilities, talents, knowledge, or time so that others can sell their products more efficiently. If you are employed, you are often selling your services to the highest bidder or to the most convenient client. You exchange your time and skills for a paycheck and benefits package. Low-skilled jobs have a lower price demand but greater availability. Higher-skilled positions require more *TAC (Training, Aptitude, Credentials)* but offer better benefits and higher pay. The steward often finds themselves serving God by serving people in an uplifting and edifying way. When working for someone, the steward should look for their niche that makes them highly valued or nearly indispensable. Be the most knowledgeable about polices, the software, the training program, or the best at customer service. Finding a niche that makes you the go-to person for that topic means the company relies on you, so that they will miss your services. Those with specialized skills can sell their services to others by working for themselves as contractors, consultants, or coordinators. Self-employment allows individuals to set their own prices, time, and workload, giving them greater control over what they will and won't do. Selling products or self-employed services means that you have a business. Even when employed, many people spend part of their time selling other services outside their 9-to-5 job to earn extra income.

SUPPLY AND DEMAND

The law of supply and demand governs the value of products and services by affecting the behavior of buyers and sellers in the market. It also affects investment habits and the availability of specific eligible programs, thereby affecting every means of earning. The amount of **SUPPLY (Stockpiling Useful Products Provides Lasting Yield)** for your product will determine the pool of customers you share with competitors. The more competition there is, the lower the price of your goods and services. However, even when there is fierce competition, the amount of **DEMAND (Desirable Effects Meets A Need Developed)** there is for that product will mitigate that effect, allowing you to increase pricing. Even if you are the only provider, if there isn't a demand for what you are selling, you won't earn much profit.

In today's society, defining success has become difficult. Many people evaluate success by material gain. The biggest problem with making money and possessions the measure of success is that many people with wealth and material possessions often find their lives unfulfilling. While success is often associated with accomplishments, the biblical picture of success is more holistic, encompassing satisfaction, contentment, and peace that come from operating in our purpose. Isaiah 26:12 says, *"Yahweh, you will ordain peace for us, for you have also done all our work for us"*. The Hebrew term Shaphath, translated as "established" or "ordained," refers to something that is set in place to transform its situation. It involves placing a pot full of water, seasoning, and spices over a fire to create a delicious stew. It reduces your life to its core elements, which are necessary for achieving peace and productivity. True success comes from the Lord. As Christians, we must recognize that all our accomplishments stem from combining the right ingredients of a good plan, hard work, and knowledge with the guidance of God, so that He will grant us success. Let's take a look at a few examples of people whom God has given success.

JOSEPH

> *Genesis 39:3-4 His master saw that Yahweh was with him, and that Yahweh made all that he did prosper in his hand. Joseph found favor in his sight. He ministered to him, and Potiphar made him overseer over his house, and all that he had he put into his hand.*

When Joseph, the son of Jacob, was 17 years old, his brothers betrayed him because of their jealousy and sold him into slavery. However, the same favor he had enjoyed while faithfully serving his father, Jacob, was still with him in Potiphar's house. Everything he did prospered in his hands. His favor stemmed from the outlook that he wasn't just serving people, but serving God. Potiphar was a seasoned official in Egypt, and he had an eye for talent. Joseph's youth and relative inexperience wouldn't prevent his promotion, because God had established the results of his labors. He worked smart, did things the right way, maintained good communication and integrity, and God therefore prospered all he did. His integrity earned him favor, but it also drew attacks because he did what was right, not just what others wanted. Potiphar's wife falsely accused him, leading to his arrest, but even in prison, he succeeded.

Genesis 39:23 The keeper of the prison didn't look after anything that was under his hand, because Yahweh was with him; and that which he did, Yahweh made it prosper.

In the Bible, we have the example of Joseph, whom Pharaoh appointed as steward of his house and of the entire nation of Egypt, where he was responsible for preparing the country for the famine. However, things started very differently for him. No one knows how many years Joseph served in Potiphar's house as opposed to how many years he served in prison. Potiphar imprisoned Joseph for over 2 years of his total 13 years of captivity as a slave and then a prisoner. However, the captain of the prison observed the same prosperity and favor that caused Potiphar not to worry about anything Joseph was in charge of. A faithful steward can prosper in the most challenging situations. However, like Joseph, we must keep our faith in God strong, our hope must be grounded, and we cannot allow hatred and regret to seep into our hearts.

DAVID

1 Samuel 18:14-16 David was successful in all his ways, for the LORD was with him. When Saul saw that he was very successful, he was afraid of him. But all Israel and Judah loved David, for he would go out to battle and return before them. (NASB)

The secret to the steward's success is that God is with them, or, more accurately, they work in tandem with God. David was not yet king, but he still caught the attention of those in positions above and below him. Why? Because he was successful in all his ways, Saul saw David as fighting for the house of Saul, but was afraid. The people saw David as fighting for the tribes of Israel and respected him. David fought for the kingdom of God, so the Lord prospered him. When you do something well, people will envy you. When your work improves others' lives, they will appreciate you. However, God is the one who prospers and protects you. Regardless of how others feel about you, it is the Lord that we are to please.

OPPRESSION STORY

> *Acts 13:17 The God of this people chose our fathers, and exalted the people when they stayed as aliens in the land of Egypt, and with an uplifted arm, he led them out of it*

Egyptian captivity leads to an exalted Israel. The reason is that God chose them. But how it happened is the real story. People struggled for generations, barely scraping by. It's not just an immigrant story; it's a story of oppression. Immigrants sometimes take generations to integrate into their new society, choosing to live in separate communities and work in or start businesses that reflect their homeland. We hear stories of migrants who have achieved success within one generation, and others about those who continue to struggle for many more generations. The first generation consists of immigrants, while the rest are citizens. However, successive generations may live with the oppressive story of what they never had. The majority of the people looked at the Israelites as foreigners who didn't quite fit into Egyptian culture. However, they had been there for generations without a fair chance. This affected how the Israelites viewed themselves.

The oppressive story is a mindset you can either accept or overcome. When you grow up in a subculture that doesn't expect to do much, you have to be the one who refuses to accept what others say about you and what your God can do. Being raised with disadvantages doesn't stop your exaltation.

You have to choose your difficulty. Going to school will be challenging, but remaining in a low-paying job will be difficult as well. Starting a business will be challenging, but working for others and watching them profit from your labor is equally difficult. Choosing your difficulty determines how successful you will be. Staying in an oppressive story is hard. Choosing to take on additional temporary hardship to reach your elevation story is also hard. But only one of these promotes you. Each generation that suffered brought growth, so when the time of the exodus came, around 70 Israelites living in Egypt became a nation. The steward's job is to trust God, doing their best as He turns their story of oppression into one of elevation.

> "The Highest vocation you can ever possibly hope to achieve is the one that God gives you. God needs people from all walks of life who are prepared to be used by Him to accomplish His purpose." – Greg Laurie.

DART PLAN FOR SETTING GOALS

Doing our best requires positioning ourselves to prosper. Prospering begins by setting goals. Goals are targets or objectives we aim to achieve. We must never forget that the most important goal we can set is to have a close relationship with God. There is a surprising way that our relationship with God and others affects our professional development and habits. A goal without a plan is just a wish. If you fail to plan, you are planning to fail. A steward takes the time to plan their work so they can be as productive as possible. If you don't have a target, you don't know what you will hit. Setting goals is one of the most effective ways to accomplish our tasks. There are three key points to consider when setting goals. Targets are hit by throwing a dart, shooting an arrow, or firing a gun. Targeting brings us to the DART method of goal setting, which means our goals should be Distinct, Achievable, Reliable, and Timely.

DISTINCT

Goals must be distinct because vague goals, such as saying "I want to be rich," are rarely achieved with integrity intact. Desire without purpose is an attempt to achieve something you want without accomplishing something good, which opens the door for carnal living. The steward always acts with a purpose. Whether the goal is a desired weight, a college degree, or the purchase of a piece of property, setting clear goals gives us something to work toward. *Proverbs 19:2 It isn't good to have zeal without knowledge, nor being hasty with one's feet and missing the way.*

ACHIEVABLE

Our goals should be achievable. It is something within our capacity, even when we have to learn new things. If there is no system or framework in place to achieve your goal, you may need to create one. If creating one is beyond your reach, you may have to wait for someone to create it or hire someone to do so. However, you can't wait too long for someone else to build something to fit your dream. That would take things too far out of your hands. We should be able to review our work and see that we are on the right path. *Zechariah 4:10 Indeed, who despises the day of small things? For these seven shall rejoice, and shall see the plumb line in the hand of Zerubbabel. These are Yahweh's eyes, which run back and forth through the whole earth.*

RELIABLE:

Our goals should be reliable, meaning that even when they are difficult, they can help us. Think about what you are doing and why you want to achieve it. We shouldn't set goals solely for the sake of having a goal, nor should we copy the goals of others that don't align with our business, vocation, or life choices. Look to accomplish what you can do. *Luke 14:28-30 "For which of you, desiring to build a tower, doesn't first sit down and count the cost, to see if he has enough to complete it? Or perhaps, when he has laid a foundation and isn't able to finish, everyone who sees begins to mock him, saying, 'This man began to build and wasn't able to finish.*

TIMELY

Our goals should have a specific completion date. We don't want to prolong things indefinitely. We should set daily goals because they make habits. Setting short-term goals provides us with markers to evaluate progress, while long-term goals represent our life vision. Work to do what God has called you to do. David didn't build the temple; his son, Solomon, did. However, he fulfilled his purpose by preparing the finances and framework needed for the future. *Acts 13:36 For David, after he had served God's purpose in his own generation, fell asleep, and was buried among his fathers and underwent decay (NASB)*

THE ARROW OF SUCCESS

1 Corinthians 3:13 Each man's work will be revealed. For the Day will declare it, because it is revealed in fire; and the fire itself will test what sort of work each man's work is.

As stewards of God, we are to do what pleases our Master. We must keep in mind that our work will be proved by God one day. Family, friends, fitness, faith, and financial freedom are essential, but the Christian steward mainly defines success as doing what pleases God. *Galatians 1:10 For am I now seeking the favor of men, or of God? Or am I striving to please men? For if I were still pleasing men, I wouldn't be a servant of Christ.* God will test each person's works, and our goal is to hit the target right in the bullseye. It is our responsibility to know what he has called us to do. As children of

God, we have a **BOW (Blessing of Wisdom)** in which to shoot our arrow, hitting the target head-on. The acronym **ARROW (Accountability, Readiness, Restraint, Opportunity, Willingness)** describes the elements that are essential for any successful endeavor. All five elements work together, building upon each other. Let's take a look at each element.

ACCOUNTABILITY

> *Galatians 6:4 But let each man examine his own work, and then he will have reason to boast in himself, and not in someone else.*

Being accountable begins with self-evaluation, followed by seeking the evaluation and assistance of someone you trust to help you progress. Self-evaluation is the initial stage where your capacity and fitness are measured. Reevaluation is the final stage of stewardship, where you assess what you have accomplished and determine whether you have achieved your goals. Failing to reach your goals is an opportunity to evaluate yourself and reassess the process, determining whether your current approach is the most effective way to achieve your set goals.

READINESS

> *Ecclesiastes 10:10 If the ax is blunt, and one doesn't sharpen the edge, then he must use more strength; but skill brings success.*

Training and preparation are necessary steps to success. Preparation involves gaining knowledge about what we do. A steward is in the employ of his master. We must recognize that, whether in the church or out of it, we are all working for God. God calls some to be the best they can be in business. Others are the best teachers, handypersons, or homemakers. Whatever you do, God requires excellence from all His stewards. We are to be the light of the world; therefore, we must prepare for that light to shine.

RESTRAINT

Proverbs 10:4 He becomes poor who works with a lazy hand, but the hand of the diligent brings wealth.

Restraint is our ability to put controls and limits on our actions. We should establish healthy parameters not only for our work but also for our rest. There is just no substitute for hard work. Pouring our energy and effort into our endeavors only makes what we do stronger. To be successful, you need a strong work ethic, and to prevent burnout, you need to find a balance between work and rest. Sowing and reaping mean that the more you put into your endeavors, the more you will take out, but even the land needs time to rest.

OPPORTUNITY

Revelations 3:8 I know your works (behold, I have set before you an open door, which no one can shut), that you have a little power, and kept my word, and didn't deny my name.

Success has more to do with timing than nearly anything else. A good opportunity can change your life, and successful people are ready when it comes.

Yet we must consider what we must give up to take the opportunity. Weighing your values before taking an opportunity is essential. Sometimes we create opportunities by seizing the occasion. When doors open, make your move, but be careful that you are ready to handle what you ask for. You step out too fast ahead of the Lord and BOOM! Everything falls apart. However, if you wait too long, someone will capitalize on the opportunity that remains open.

WILLINGNESS

Psalms 20:4 May He grant you your heart's desire And fulfill your whole plan! (NASB)

If you ever wonder about your call, the first thing to check is what you are passionate about. To truly be successful, we need to do something that we enjoy and are passionate about, something that we are willing to dedicate ourselves to. Note: We should never confuse our God given passion with the sinful lust of our hearts. Ephesians 3:10 says that God created us for good works, which God prepared in advance for us to do. God prepared the work for us. Then, God gave us the desire to do the work He prepared for us. To follow your passion is to follow the will of God for your life. However, even the things we desire require our willingness. We experience competing desires that may conflict, leading us to choose one over the other. That's where willingness takes hold and takes over.

THE GUN WORK ETHIC

Colossians 3:23 And whatever you do, work heartily, as for the Lord and not for men.

The third thing people use to hit a target is a gun. **GUN (Giving, Understanding, Nurturing)** is an acronym describing our work ethic. The GUN is something you aim, but the **BULLET (Balanced Understanding Leaves Labor Eradicating Targets)** hits the target. Brother Lawrence, a 17th-century French Monk, once said. *"The issue is not the needful that we should have great things to do… We can do little things for God; when I turn a cake that is frying in a pan for love of Him, and that done, if there is nothing else to call me, I prostrate myself in worship before Him who has given me grace to work."* Our work is work-ship when we acknowledge and involve God at every point. Work-ship is what the priest does when offering the sacraments. He is working, but it is an act of worship. It doesn't matter what kind of work we do. Whether we are in business for ourselves or work for someone else, we are to work as if God employed us. Working with God inspires us to do our best, enabling us to achieve our target goals. Let's take a quick minute to review the GUN work ethic.

GROWTH

By growth, I mean giving yourself to your work. Steven A. Smith said, "Champions do daily what others do occasionally". Hard work means you are showing up for yourself and your vision. Chances are, if you work harder than your competition, you will get better results. The employed steward should always work hard enough to exceed company norms and expectations. However, we should note that working hard as an employee when you have managers with no vision may sometimes lead to being overlooked, as you become so valuable in a lower position that you become indispensable to their department. Your individual goals and expectations should always be kept in mind when working at a company that doesn't value internal promotions. However, working hard for yourself is another story. All your hard work benefits you. Here are four principles about the importance of hard work.

1. **Hard Work shows Wisdom:** Proverbs 6:6-8 Go to the ant, you sluggard. Consider her ways, and be wise; which, having no chief, overseer, or ruler, provides her bread in the summer, and gathers her food in the harvest.
2. **Hard Work leads to Increase:** Proverbs 14:23 In all hard work there is profit, but the talk of the lips leads only to poverty.
3. **Hard work brings Reward:** Proverbs 12:14 A man shall be satisfied with good by the fruit of his mouth. The work of a man's hands shall be rewarded to him.
4. **Hard Work brings Promotion:** Proverbs 22:29 Do you see a man skilled in his work? He will serve kings. He won't serve obscure men.

UNDERSTANDING

Working hard is good; working smart is better. As stewards, we should continually strive towards our vision and concept for our lives. Opinions on reading for expertise vary, but to gain general knowledge of a topic, reading three well-rounded books on the subject is generally required. Start by making this a six-month goal. In two years, reading ten books on the topic should allow you to understand the consensus of experts and place you in the top 10% of people with knowledge in the field. Within four years, reading 20 books on the subject will give you expert-level knowledge, leading you to be sought after for instruction, interviews, advice, and tips on the topic. Many people benefit from this type of autodidactic learning and become leaders in their fields without a formal education. It is crucial to apply that knowledge as you progress to gain expert-level experience, complementing the knowledge you have already acquired. How you market this information and turn it into a profitable venture is up to you. Knowledge is essential to thrive. We have all seen people run their businesses on life support, simply doing the old things they were taught, without any new thought or innovation. It may work for them, but achieving excellence requires moving to the next level. Knowing how to function in business is not the same as knowing how to flourish.

NURTURING

I hope you didn't think I had forgotten my earlier statement about how our relationships with God and others influence our professional development and habits. Healthy, well-balanced personal relationships lead to a significant increase in self-confidence, greater job satisfaction, enhanced productivity, and improved overall performance. Good personal relations tend to lead to better mental health, with sound support systems and a springboard for releasing stress. The higher level of joy and motivation from good relationships increases our productivity, and the communication skills we develop lead to networking opportunities for more satisfying options. Not only will good relationships reflect in our attitudes, but they also cause us to set healthy boundaries governing our time and energy.

SAVING NOT HOARDING

Proverbs 13:11 "Dishonest money dwindles away, but he who gathers money little by little makes it grow". (NIV)

One of the simplest measures of success is the ability to **SAVE (Securing A Valuable Early)** money. Saving means your income exceeds your expenses. Unfortunately, this isn't a reality for everyone. No one wants to live paycheck to paycheck, yet many struggle to save money. Surveys indicate that people would rather discuss their weight than their savings. It can be unpleasant to realize you can't afford to save a little. While both saving and hoarding involve storing up, there is a significant difference between them. Saving is the act of storing money for a specific purpose. Hoarding is the act of storing up for fear or selfish pride. There is wisdom in starting a savings plan. It doesn't matter how little you save, whether it's $5, $20, or $100 a month. Over time, what you put away will become a source of great riches for you.

> *Psalms 17:14 From men by your hand, Yahweh, from men of the world, whose portion is in this life. You fill the belly of your cherished ones. Your sons have plenty, and they store up wealth for their children.*

Success without a successor is a failure that has not yet happened. We save not only to finance our dreams and future, but also to give our family a leg up, which is why home ownership is a crucial goal. It is a method of saving. A home is a savings investment, even when you don't have money in a traditional sense to save. Purchasing a home is not easy, as it costs more than renting. However, after around ten years of ownership, rent increases generally catch up to what you may have been paying for your mortgage. Then, after twenty years, you may be paying less on your mortgage than people who rent pay for an apartment. Home prices also increase, allowing homeowners to build equity they can cash out on in their lifetimes or pass on to their children as an inheritance. After living in a home for 40 years, the equity could have doubled or more. The people we bought our home from moved to Virginia when home prices were almost half those in the Los Angeles area. They used the sale price to purchase their new home, paying the full price and having money left over to help supplement their retirement. It was a good plan. Passing the home down to your children or grandchildren is also a good plan. However, you must place your home in a living trust for them to avoid the lengthy probate process and capital gains tax.

DOING THE LORD'S BUSINESS

This section is more for small church leaders. While pastoring a church in Southern California, I encountered a dilemma while reading the parable of the talents. Our church funds were kept solely in a business checking account because it was the simplest way to store and record them. Typically, you want to save enough to cover three to six months of expenses before doing anything else with money, but we were saving money to purchase our first building and were well beyond that. Reading about the steward who buried his master's money in the ground, I thought about Matthew 25:26-27, which says, *"But his lord answered him, 'You wicked and slothful servant." You knew that I reap where I didn't sow, and gather where I didn't scatter. You ought therefore to have deposited my money with the bankers, and at my coming I should have received back my own with interest.*

My problem was that, though my method of saving was safe and funds were federally insured, it was equivalent to burying the Lord's money in the ground. I was the unjust steward because we earned no interest, and that had to change. *2 Corinthians 5:9 says, "Therefore also we make it our aim, whether at home or absent, to be well pleasing to him."* I had not done my best when God had done His best for me. We placed the funds in a certificate of deposit (CD) that was both safe and federally insured, earning interest. Suppose your church had $100,000 invested in a CD that earned 5% interest per year. After a year, you would have an additional $5,000. What you earn is like gaining a few more contributors to the church, which grows the Lord's funds. However, as the stewards of the Lord's money, we can't gamble with what the people give in stocks or annuities, as that would also be unjust. But the people didn't give the $5,000 increase. The increase can be allocated to higher-yield investments, allowing for gradual growth in funds to support the Lord's work. This way, we protect what the people have given while doing business in the name of the Lord.

THE ABCS OF SUCCESS

· · · · ·

Achieving the abundant life where Christ is your goal.

Being a good person by treating others with love

Considering those who are essential in your life

Doing something uncomfortable to make a better future

Earning enough to support your life and family

Forgiveness from a heart of grace

Giving with a cheerful heart

Healing from past hurts

Increasing in favor with God and man

Joy in our hearts

Keeping God's commandments

Loving others like Christ loved you

Making memories that will last a lifetime

Never giving up

Operating in the gifts and talents given to you

Pleasing the Lord

Quiet time where God restores your soul

Resisting sinful urges and casting away sinful thoughts

Saving for the Future

Time used wisely

Understanding God's plan for your life

Valuing what you have

Waiting with wisdom and patience

X-amining yourself to see if you are in the faith

Yielding your heart and mind to the Lord

Zealously pursuing your goal

Scan for video on: The Abundant Life

CHAPTER THREE

SERVICE OVER SENTIMENT

· · · · · · · · · · · · ·

MATTHEW 10:16

Behold, I send you out as sheep among wolves. Therefore
be wise as serpents and harmless as doves.

A lthough this chapter discusses the disposition and duties of a
Christian steward, it does not begin by highlighting the loving
heart and concern that believers should have. It's not that we won't get
there, but that's usually where people start and finish. Instead, we will
start with strategy. Service over sentiment is the concept that we do not
always act in our own self-interest. Sometimes this is because the believer
is to act selflessly, giving of themselves. At other times, our sentimentality
is not strategic. When Christ sends out the apostles and instructs them to
be as wise as serpents, He wasn't referring to the sinful association with
the serpent in Genesis, but instead to the strategic habits of a snake. The
apostles were going to a new territory and should be aware that when a
serpent goes somewhere new, it first scouts out the land. The snake searches

for hiding spots, such as holes and rocks in open areas, to avoid predators. It looks for where its prey gathers, but doesn't attack unless it has the full lay of the land. It is a dog-eat-sheep world we operate in, and Jesus instructs us to be strategic but safe.

A steward takes care of something by essentially standing in for someone else, requiring the steward to operate not according to their own heart, but according to the heart of the one they serve. A company steward is a business manager who oversees the owner's operations, handling tasks on the owner's behalf. When we live as God's stewards, our **SERVICE (Servant Eagerly Ready Visualize In Caring Efforts)** must exceed the sentimentalities of our hearts. Jeremiah 17:9 says, *"The heart is deceitful above all things and it is exceedingly corrupt. Who can know it?"* There may be times when what you think is best is not what God is leading you to do. What we are to do in those situations is follow the Lord's lead. We sometimes bail people out when God needed them to go through a situation to break their pride and challenge them to address the sin in their lives. Without discernment, sentimentality is a toxic trait. It opens you up to people's sinister motives and manipulation. A steward must know when to say no and when someone is trying to manipulate them. The enemy tries to weaponize our hearts, either by closing them off, making us selfish and unconcerned, or by exploiting our sensitivity, which wears us out in our attempts to save the world.

Sentimentality isn't always about the other person. Sometimes it's about the things we won't let go. Downsizing so you can save or pay off bills is a good strategy, but holding onto too much during downsizing can slow or hinder your progress. A friend of mine downsized and stored a lot of items in two storage units while living with family. Storage rent for two units costs them $314 a month, so they can keep their furniture, which they estimate is worth about $4,000. However, they lived with their family for two years. You can do the math. Not only did they have the hassle of going to the unit monthly to make payments, which took a lot of their time, but they also paid $7,536 to keep and store $4,000 worth of furniture. Perhaps they could have sold the furniture for half its value, applied the money to their debt, and come out with brand-new furniture when they moved two years later.

> *Proverbs 21:2 Every way of a man is right in his own eyes, but Yahweh weighs the hearts.*

Strategy alone is not enough. Although it may seem right, we must be concerned about living with both right motives and actions. Some acts are not generosity, they are ingenuity, as the tit for tat expectation of achieving something greater in return is present. As Christians, we must be faithful to God's plan and to what He has given us while maintaining a heart and attitude of gratitude. Stewardship is not a short-term commitment that we change our minds about later when things don't go as planned. Stewardship is not about pride in performance, seeking a position, or recognition. Stewardship is service from the heart, driven by love. We must stay mindful and focused, living our lives led by God's Spirit.

Consider the vision you have for your life. Not only does it have a hopeful ending, but it also features the solid character of the person you are trying to become. Vision doesn't have to be grandiose. Most people's vision has them fulfilling the mandate in 1 Thessalonians 4:11, which reads: *"That you also aspire to lead a quiet life, to mind your own business, and to work with your own hands, as we commanded you."* In your vision, what kind of person are you in the life you lead? You may see yourself as more prosperous, more peaceful, but also more personable with greater moral characteristics. The steward's character matters because people make the most crucial decisions about your future when you're not in the room. Your character speaks for you when you're not around, and God will speak for you because of your character.

A mentor taught me the qualities I would need to be a proper steward. Yes, we should have mentors. They said that a steward's role is to commit our work to the Lord, but we need to have a right mind. Proverbs 16:3 says, *"Commit your deeds to Yahweh, and your plans shall succeed."* We work from, to, and with our commitment to God. I say from, because God gives us purpose, to, because we are serving Him, and with, because we are working together with the Lord in His plan. The next thing needed is fear and reverence for God. Proverbs 14:26 reads *"In the fear of Yahweh is a secure fortress, and he will be a refuge for his children."* This kind of reverence will cause you not to make life decisions lightly, but instead to trust God. I learned never to make a life decision when I was anxious, angry, or afraid. Emotions will cause your greatest **MISTAKE (Misguided Inaccurate Steps That Allow Key Errors)**. The last thing said was that I needed to follow the plan without deviation to receive the reward. Too many of us abandon our plan when things aren't coming soon enough. *Whoever despises instruction will pay for it, but he who respects a command will be rewarded (Proverbs 13:13).* We can learn from the wisdom and experience of those who took the hard lumps and lived to talk about it, or we can ignore their wisdom only to get a few lumps ourselves.

A CLEAR AND CARNAL EXAMPLE

Jesus needed a steward to handle the ministry finances. Matthew, previously known as Levi the tax collector, would have been an obvious choice. Why not have the IRS agent who joined the ministry handle the finances? Yet he likely didn't want to serve where he sinned. Loving money was the root of Matthew's sin until he found a greater love in the Lord. Churches tend not to allow someone who is spiritually immature and struggling financially onto the finance team, specifically because it would increase their temptation to succumb to covetousness. So, instead of Matthew, Judas took care of the money bag and made arrangements for the ministry. Judas Iscariot became the steward for Jesus Christ personally and the apostles as a group. When people wanted to give to support Christ's ministry, everyone pointed to Judas to receive it. He was so adept at raising money that he knew the value of oiled perfume in a woman's alabaster jar. Judas shared in the teaching, ministry, and fellowship of the apostles, yet, according to John 12:6, he continually embezzled the money. Judas was a poor steward not only of the finances but also of his heart and relationship with God. He didn't just suddenly betray Jesus for 30 pieces of silver. He had been betraying Jesus for silver all along. He just used the Passover to get himself a bigger payday. How many of us are close to divine truth but aren't listening? Like Judas, some things can compromise our hearts and lives as stewards. Let's look at a few.

WICKEDNESS:

> *Proverbs 10:7 The memory of the righteous is blessed, but the name of the wicked will rot.*

Just because things look good on the outside doesn't mean they're not falling apart from within. Deception makes things appear healthy at first glance, but when people look a little deeper, they discover the truth. A wicked servant does not belong to God; they belong to themselves. Like the devil, some people want to enjoy the ride until the end. Many will keep going until someone or something stops them.

SELF-ADORATION:

> *Proverbs 27:2 Let another man praise you, and not your own mouth; a stranger, and not your own lips.*

There is nothing wrong with tooting your own horn a little, but when it gets too loud, you can't see or hear what you need. Focusing on ourselves takes our focus away from the Lord we serve. Think of the person on social media who constantly checks their posts to see who liked or responded.

Take that person somewhere to talk to them, and they will be distracted by what flatters them. The problem is that praise may make you feel good, but correction will help you become a better person. When others see the best version of you, you won't need to praise yourself; they will do it for you.

HATRED:

Proverbs 26:24 A malicious man disguises himself with his lips, but he harbors evil in his heart.

Believers are to be blessers, meaning we have no room for hate in our hearts. Hate causes us to miss opportunities and avoid connections God wanted us to make. Consider the first-century manual on church services, written around 90 AD, known as the Didache (Teaching of the Twelve). It instructs the early church to pray the Lord's Prayer three times a day. If we were to pray out loud daily, "Forgive our sins as we forgive those who sin against us," our minds would be so prepared to forgive that we would be offering forgiveness even before they had a chance to offend us.

CONCEALED SIN:

Proverbs 28:13 He who conceals his sins doesn't prosper, but whoever confesses and renounces them finds mercy.

Hidden sin is like bait we leave on a trap that the enemy can spring at any time. The devil will enable you to become more prosperous, excel in your endeavors, and gain more from them because he enjoys taking people down from high places. He fell from a high place and tempted Jesus to jump from a high place (Matthew 4:5-6). Concealment means you're not dealing with your sins, and that never comes out well. When we confess, we come into agreement with God, and when we renounce sin, we move from a state of fear to one of empowerment and favor.

GOD'S BEST STEWARD

Acts 4:27 For truly, both Herod and Pontius Pilate, with the Gentiles and the people of Israel, were gathered together against your holy servant Jesus, whom you anointed.

Jesus Christ is the anointed one who serves God. Those unfamiliar with Christianity think that Christ is a last name, but it's not. Christ comes from the Greek word Christos, which is a translation of the Hebrew word for Messiah, meaning "anointed one." Christ is the title for the one who carries the three anointed roles in the Old Testament: prophet, priest, and king. Jesus was the Father's steward on earth, coming to do His will (John 6:38). In His ministry, He preached the kingdom of God, healed the sick, cast out demons, and gathered disciples. It was all acting on behalf of the Father. Jesus rescued people from the storm on the Father's behalf and raised them from the dead with the Father working His will through Him. In John 5:19-20, it reads, *Jesus therefore answered them, 'Most certainly, I tell you, the Son can do nothing of himself, but what he sees the Father doing. For whatever things he does, these the Son also does likewise. For the Father has affection for the Son, and shows him all things that he himself does. He will show him greater works than these, that you may marvel."* Jesus reveals that He does nothing alone but only does what he sees the Father doing. His greater works were the result of His greater vision. God must be in our decisions and actions.

Christ's stewardship is one of completion. He admitted, *"I can of myself do nothing. As I hear, I judge; and my judgment is righteous, because I don't* seek my own will, but the will of my Father who sent me (John 5:30)." It is not that Jesus was inept at His job; when He said He could do nothing, He meant that He would not do anything without the Father. He listens to the Fathers as a source that is outside of Him yet inside Him. We, too, have the Father as an outside source, but one living inside us through His Holy Spirit. Accurate decisions come from hearing and doing what the Father says. Ignoring God for your own thoughts of getting ahead may seem temporarily advantageous, but it will remove your hedge of protection. Jesus said, *"He who sent me is with me. The Father hasn't left me alone, for I always do the things that are pleasing to him (John 8:29)."* The promise of the presence of God is in doing what pleases Him. Though His Spirit is permanently with us, His favor might not be. Our hedge grows as we operate in faithfulness, and we will need it for our future.

As stewards, it's not just about us; God has given us a work to finish. John 5:36 reads, *"But the testimony which I have is greater than that of John; for the works which the Father gave me to accomplish, the very works that I do, testify about me, that the Father has sent me."* What we do reveals who we follow, and what we complete shows how faithful we are at following. Many of us quit before we get to our tipping point. The tipping point is the moment when you pour a drink, and the coffee or tea comes out. The less full the **POTS (*Potential Often Takes Sacrifice*)**, the more you have to tip it. We may have done the right things, but we drew back just as God was about to take something from our pots. The Cross was the tipping point for Christ. God fulfilled His plan as Jesus was both the steward and the sacrifice.

7 WORDS OF STEWARDSHIP FROM THE CROSS

1. Giving Forgiveness to the undeserved - *Luke 23:34 (Father, forgive them, for they know not what they do)*
2. Bringing meaning out of hardship - *Luke 23:43 (Today you will be with me in Paradise)*
3. Caring for your family - *John 19:26 (Woman, behold, your son!)*

4. Bringing Understanding of God's Plan ~ *Matthew 27:46 (My God, my God, why have you forsaken me?)*
5. Filling those in need of His goodness ~ *John 19:28 (I thirst)*
6. Paying the debt of our sin ~ *John 19:30 (It is finished)*
7. Total trust in God ~ *Luke 23:46 (Father, into your hands I commit my spirit!)*

Taken together, we can say that Jesus' stewardship brought about a result that we did not deserve (1) and gave meaning to our hardships (2), so that we can ensure our families are taken care of (3). Understanding God's plan (4) will fill us with the things we truly need (5), removing our debt and the things that are against us (6) as we totally commit ourselves to the Lord (7).

OUR DUTY

The stewards' **DUTY (Doing Unique Tasks Yourself)** is to manage their lives effectively to achieve better outcomes. As stewards, God calls us to be compassionate caretakers and caregivers, content in Christ. As Christians, we ought to support all obedient saints and assist those who are enduring hardships in life, even if they have hardened their hearts. We can be good stewards by identifying when someone is in need and assisting when necessary. God did not invite us to disparage one another by our words or deeds, to criticize the way we behave, communicate, or even present ourselves. Because we are the Body of Christ, God has called us to love one another. Encourage people to be faithful in their commitments as they strive to be good stewards of God's many blessings by doing their best to steward life.

12 TOPICS (T'S) OF STEWARDSHIP

The primary reason you are probably reading this book is to gain a solid understanding of stewardship, which will enable you to improve your skills. We are stewards over everything that God has placed under our control. The twelve topics, or T's, of Stewardship represent the scope of responsibilities we must balance.

OUR TIME

Ephesians 5:15-16 Therefore watch carefully how you walk, not as unwise, but as wise, redeeming the time, because the days are evil.

Time is the great equalizer because we all receive the same amount each day. It is free, but priceless. You can't own it, but you spend it doing something at each moment. How we use our time will determine our productivity. Time is the constant point in life's juggling act, where we manage our time, energy, resources, and responsibilities, allocating a portion of time to each area of life to ensure we are well-balanced. Wisely used time leads to rewards from work, revitalization during learning, refreshment through enjoyment, and restoration when resting; however, wasted time is a trap that exposes us to temptation.

OVER TALENTS

1 Peter 4:10 As each has received a gift, employ it in serving one another, as good managers of the grace of God in its various forms.

Whether grand or simple, our **TAGS (*Talents, Abilities, Gifts, Skills*)** are the marks of our stewardship and will determine if we are good and faithful stewards. Talents are natural predispositions that we are born with and can use. Abilities are the capacities that shape and contain our talents, gifts, and skills. Gifts are things that come from God's grace and assist us in serving others. Skills are the honing and development of our natural talents and God given gifts. Everything begins with our talents, but we are not to end there. As we build on our natural strengths through learning and practicing them rightly, God will bless them divinely, so our abilities aren't limited to us but are enhanced by His grace, allowing us to succeed.

OUR TREASURES

Matthew 25:21 His lord said to him, 'Well done, good and faithful servant. You have been faithful over a few things, I will set you over many things. Enter into the joy of your lord.'

Treasures are valuable things. We have personal treasures consisting of things that are valuable to us because they hold importance. As children of God, we are the Father's treasures, important to His heart. Those things are cherished, not stewarded. The treasures we steward are things that we earn, trade for, or inherit. These are things that build our financial stability and responsibility. The bulk of this book will instruct on how to steward these things.

OUR TEMPLE

1 Corinthians 6:19-20 Or don't you know that your body is a temple of the Holy Spirit who is in you, whom you have from God? You are not your own, for you were bought with a price. Therefore glorify God in your body and in your spirit, which are God's.

Health and fitness are a kingdom responsibility. Jesus' healing ministry confirmed the words that He spoke. However, he did not heal with the expectation that we would not take care of ourselves afterwards. Desiring healing without pursuing healthy practices is contrary to the reason we desire healing. God has chosen to inhabit the bodies of believers and call us His temple. Ensuring the temple remains in pristine condition is cardinal. It's as simple as watching what we eat, staying active, and keeping harmful things out of our bodies, but as tricky as dealing with emotional eating, lack of motivation, self-medicating, and poor coping skills.

OUR THOUGHTS

2 Corinthians 10:5 throwing down imaginations and every high thing that is exalted against the knowledge of God and bringing every thought into captivity to the obedience of Christ,

Of course, we are stewards of our thoughts. You are the man or woman placed in charge of the house, and your body is the temple of the Holy Spirit. Your body is also God's dwelling, so your responsibility as a steward extends to several aspects of your body. Specific thoughts are either unhelpful or do not originate from you. We must steward our thoughts, accepting what is true, holy, and beneficial and rejecting deception, falsehood, and unclean thoughts. Proper thinking is essential not only because it gives us peace, but also because it shapes our beliefs. Beliefs shape our convictions, and convictions shape our attitude, which in turn influences our perceptions. Controlling thoughts limits temptation and prevents us from making poor decisions.

OUR TESTIMONY

> *Revelation 12:11 They overcame him because of the Lamb's blood, and because of the word of their testimony. They didn't love their life, even to death.*

We have two testimonies to **SHARE (Spiritually Hopeful Attitude Repeatedly Encourages)**: ours and the testimony of Christ, which we refer to as the gospel. The gospel is the good news of the propitiatory death, burial, and resurrection of our Lord. It is good news because it proclaims victory over sin and death, and its benefits are available to us. It embraces Christ's struggles, surrender, and subsequent victory. Our testimony is a personal reflection on how the gospel has empowered us to be living stones and witnesses to Christ. Stewarding our testimony requires us to live closely to Christ's word and be a good representative of Him in the world. The more we share our testimony and link it to Christ, the greater the impact we will have on others' faith.

OUR TREATMENT

> *Romans 13:10 Love doesn't harm a neighbor. Love therefore is the fulfillment of the law.*

One of the most apparent signs of Christian conversion is a life of love. Out of the 100 "One Another" passages in the New Testament, there are 59 clear commands expressing how we are to treat (or not treat) each other. Loving one another doesn't mean we should make the gospel social, focusing merely on how to help others. It does mean that we should consider more than ourselves in the decisions we make and the issues we support. We may not always be treated in life as well as we treat others, but the steward serves God by serving His people and will reap great rewards in the end.

OUR TRUST

> *Proverbs 3:5 Trust in Yahweh with all your heart, and don't lean on your own understanding.*

A good steward does things the way his master desires. Trust reveals your patterns for dealing with complications. The key meaning of the word "faith" is to trust; therefore, having faith in God is equivalent to trusting Him. Our **TRUST (*Total Reliance Upon Spiritual Truth*)** in God won't let us down. It means not taking shortcuts or exploiting situations that could benefit you but would compromise your integrity. It also means trusting God when you don't understand what He is doing or how things will work out. People found that God would not do miracles among them because they lacked faith and trust. We steward our trust so that God will do more in our lives than we expected.

OUR THEOLOGY

> *1 Thessalonians 5:21 Test all things, and hold firmly that which is good.*

Theology refers to our understanding of God, and a steward's top priority is God. They are first children of God, then disciples, and, after gaining knowledge and responsibility, they can become good stewards. Discipleship leads to stewardship and comprises three tiers that must be balanced and maintained. These tiers are orthodoxy (correct teaching), orthopraxy (correct practices), and orthopathy (a right heart). In other words, we must ensure that our head, hands, and heart are right with God. If the steward drifts from the faith that was once for all handed down to us, then they are out of alignment with the will of God.

OUR TEMPER

Ephesians 4:26-27 Be angry, and don't sin." Don't let the sun go down on your wrath, and don't give place to the devil

There is nothing wrong with getting angry, but staying angry means you are out of balance. Benjamin Franklin said, "Anything begun in anger ends in shame." A steward must always reason before making any moves, but anger will have us responding emotionally instead. A person not in control of their emotions is not in control of their thinking. Have you ever noticed that you cannot see your reflection in a pot of boiling water? In the same way, anger mars our ability to reflect God's image. Why? Because anger shuts our ears to God and opens the door to the devil. Anger is usually a cover for pain and frustration. Anger doesn't solve problems; it only exacerbates existing issues.

OUR THANKFULNESS

1 Thessalonians 5:18 In everything give thanks, for this is the will of God in Christ Jesus toward you.

A steward is grateful for their position, possessions, and the provision it affords. A thankful heart is a humble heart. Humility and gratitude are two sides of the same coin, bringing us fulfillment and contentment. Humility receives with contentment. Gratitude gives back to God with joy. This joyful contentment brings peace to our hearts. We should never discount the power of an attitude of gratitude. It draws God near and chases trouble away. In the midst of us waiting for a breakthrough, God is waiting for a thank you for the past things and the things He has yet to do.

OUR TONGUE

Matthew 12:36-37 I tell you that every idle word that men speak, they will give account of it in the day of judgment. For by your words you will be justified, and by your words you will be condemned."

Our words and deeds make a difference in our world. Words are judgments revealing our thoughts and character. God calls us to be the most loving people on the earth, but our words can be condemning. Careless speech can damage the human soul, driving others away from God, when we should be drawing them near. As a representative of God, the steward's words matter. However, it's not only about the words you speak over others, but also about the words you speak over yourself. We are responsible for not speaking damaging words about others and ourselves. Self-condemnation stemming from guilt and shame deprecates the soul because it is not a godly conviction, and therefore does not lead us to the repentance that frees our souls.

Proper use of the 12 T's requires that we use each in cooperation for the glory of God and the betterment of our future. Everything we do for and with God will eventually benefit us. He has given us 12 things to manage, trusting Him for the increase. We aren't just using these things; we are putting them to their intended purpose. We trust in God, who cannot possibly mismanage our lives worse than we have done ourselves. That is the heart and key to being God's steward.

If there is an additional "T" to the twelve, I would say that the church has the stewardship of thetokens of Eucharistic communion. Jesus speaks to the apostles in Luke 22:19-20, which says, *"He took bread, and when he had given thanks, he broke and gave it to them, saying, 'This is my body which is given for you. Do this in memory of me." 20Likewise, he took the cup after supper, saying, "This cup is the new covenant in my blood, which is poured out for you."* The Eucharist derives from the Greek word eukaristos, meaning "gratitude" or "thanksgiving." Jesus takes the tokens of bread and wine and gives them as gifts to His people to celebrate and memorialize His sacrifice on the cross. The Eucharist is stewardship celebrated and is the heart of New Testament worship; Christ placed the tokens in the hands of His church to steward His presence. The church is to handle this responsibility with a serious attitude and deliver the tokens that have been blessed and given thanks over to Christ's people.

THE WIDOWS' MITES, A TALE OF TRIUMPH OR TRAGEDY

· · · · ·

Luke 21:1-4 He looked up and saw the rich people who were putting their gifts into the treasury. He saw a certain poor widow casting in two small brass coins. He said, "Truly I tell you, this poor widow put in more than all of them, for all these put in gifts for God from their abundance, but she, out of her poverty, put in all that she had to live.

The story of the widow who gave all she had has inspired many to be faithful givers. Jesus acknowledged her giving in a way that shows that small gifts can be greater than large ones. His example doesn't mention any future rewards she would receive. Jesus gave the context in the words He said immediately before stating, *"Beware of those scribes who like to walk in long robes, and love greetings in the marketplaces, the best seats in the synagogues, and the best places at feasts; who devour widows' houses, and for a pretense make long prayers. These will receive greater condemnation* (Luke 20:46-47)."

Immediately after speaking about how scribes devour widows' houses, this widow gives all she has to live on. The woman did more than the law required; she gave it all. She would have nothing to eat or survive on, which would basically devour her house. Spiritual manipulation was so common that it happened as quickly as Christ said it. All Jesus had to do was go to the treasury and wait for a while, and it would happen. It shows why we have been experts in teaching people to sow without showing them how to reap. When we speak of her triumph in believing in God, we should remember the tragedy Christ witnessed. She had rich people among her, yet she remained poor. It's a double tragedy, revealing the scribes' manipulation of God's word and the indifference of the rich who gave from their abundance. It is also a double triumph because God saw her, and she has inspired us to be givers.

Scan to watch video: Discernment and Decision Making

CHAPTER FOUR

EVERY GOOD ENDEAVOR

. . . .

As a pastor, I realize that some leaders are unafraid to discuss money but become overbearing and even gimmicky in their encouragement of giving. Other leaders shy away from the responsibility of teaching about money, not wanting to appear greedy or taxing the people. There needs to be a balance where people are taught not only about giving, but also about the stewardship of every area of their lives. Recently, the men's fellowship of our church formed a subgroup for those interested in learning about investing. It happened naturally and organically, as the men who trade and invest just wanted to share the information they had with others. We have people in the church who work in credit repair, financing, logistics, and those who have learned about investing, who can share the wealth of their knowledge. However, for years, they had not discussed these things.

Though I have taught stewardship, there are things these men know that I am learning from them. You don't realize what you didn't know until you begin to learn more. Just as I have mentors, they have mentors too. The people you may need to grow and develop may be sitting right next to you. I believe God is shifting the season so that churches become places where financial literacy and stewardship are as foundational as other values within the church. We must be willing to learn, as financial stewardship is one of the most important spiritual and moral issues of our day. Financial and economic development is the missing piece that the Lord wants to use to bring the next generation back into His church, as well as what we need to foster the development of those already in the church.

In Chapter One on kingdom stewardship, I mentioned that, as Stewards of God, we are not owners but managers of God's resources. It is the manager's responsibility to handle their boss's business affairs, or, in our case, the local affairs of the Sovereign Lord of the Universe. God has many business ventures He desires to fund. Some of these ventures include running local ministries, worldwide evangelism, caring for the needy, promoting personal and social development, providing educational resources, and offering legal recourse, to name a few. God funds these ventures by redistributing His resources from the hands of private stewards to those of local, charitable, or ecclesial stewarding organizations.

SEEDTIME AND HARVEST

> *Genesis 8:22 While the earth remains, seed time and harvest, and cold and heat, and summer and winter, and day and night will not cease."*

Seedtime and Harvest, or sowing and reaping time, is God's method of redistributing and then replenishing wealth for kingdom purposes. As we sow into the kingdom of God, we are, in fact, taking the wealth and resources that belong to Him and transferring them to fund His work. Reaping is God's method of replenishing His wealth and supplying back to His servants for being faithful with their financial responsibilities. Sowing and reaping have been called the Law of Reciprocity, which is giving back for what someone gave to you. Sowing and reaping form a perfect continuous cycle of supply and demand, or, to put it more accurately, demand and supply. The demand for something always governs the supply. When God demands something, the steward supplies it. The reason for this demand is reciprocity. Genesis 2:8 says, *"Yahweh God planted a garden eastward, in Eden, and there he put the man whom he had formed"*. Sowing did not start with humanity but with God. We entered into what the Lord has sown. As humans, we began at the reaping stage, consuming what grew naturally and then caring for what remained, with Genesis 2:15 saying, *"Yahweh God took the man, and put him into the garden of Eden to cultivate and keep it. Yahweh God commanded the man, saying, You may freely eat of every tree of the garden."*

SOWING

Sowing is the process of taking what we have and distributing it to see something greater in return. The return is usually not immediate, but over time, it will become a harvest. Sowing takes patience. Jesus said, *"Most certainly I tell you, unless a grain of wheat falls into the earth and dies, it remains by itself alone. But if it dies, it bears much fruit" (John 12:24).* Every living thing that God created has a way of reproducing. Whether it reproduces by falling to the ground and dying or by procreation, everything alive will multiply.

> *1 Corinthians 15:36-38 You foolish one, that which you yourself sow is not made alive unless it dies. That which you sow, you don't sow the body that will be, but a bare grain, maybe of wheat, or of some other kind. But God gives it a body even as it pleased him, and to each seed a body of its own.*

This principle is key to understanding sowing. If you understand that God gave everything with life the ability to multiply, then you can understand that this multiplication comes from planting seeds. As you plant a **SEED (Shell Encouraging Entities Development)**, you will see growth, and after growth comes multiplication. Listen to what the following verses tell us about how God made what is living to reproduce after itself.

- **Genesis 1:11** God said, "Let the earth yield grass, herbs yielding seeds, and fruit **trees bearing fruit after their kind**, with their seeds in it, on the earth;" and it was so
- **Genesis 1:21** God created the large sea creatures and every **living creature that** moves, with which the waters **swarmed, after their kind**, and every winged **bird after its kind**. God saw that it was good.
- **Genesis 1:24** God said, "Let the earth produce **living creatures after their kind**, livestock, creeping things, and animals of the earth after their kind;" and it was so.

All life originated from a cell, spore, seed, or egg, not from space, but from God. All life is a living resource created by God for a purpose, but corrupted by sin. As stewards, we are also God's resources. All living resources produce after their own kind. Understanding the environment in which they grow and how to foster that growth leads to their increased productivity. The same principles apply to nonliving resources, such as financial assets, real and intellectual property, and natural resources. Learning how to use things correctly and causing whatever excess you have left to grow is the key to good stewardship.

WHAT TO SOW

Everything that has life can grow and reproduce. God's ordained method of causing things to reproduce begins with the act of sowing. Ecclesiastes

11:4 *says, "He who observes the wind won't sow; and he who regards the clouds won't reap."* With nothing sown, nothing is reaped. One of the first principles I learned in taking Economics 101 was **TANSTAAFL (There Ain't No Such Thing As A Free Lunch).** Someone has to pay the price, even if they give it away for free. The steward who wishes to reap a harvest for the Master must know what to sow and how to sow. Let us define what we mean by sowing. Sowing is the act of depositing a **SAT (Substance, Action, or Thought)** into a natural, social, or spiritual environment. There are, therefore, three different types of materials with which we sow, which we sometimes refer to as seed. There are also three different venues or environments into which we implant this material. By sowing the right material into the right environment, the steward begins the process of becoming fruitful with the master's substance.

> *Galatians 6:7-8 Don't be deceived. God is not mocked, for whatever a man sows, that he will also reap. For he who sows to his own flesh will from the flesh reap corruption. But he who sows to the Spirit will from the Spirit reap eternal life.*

SOWING A SUBSTANCE

By sowing a substance, we are referring to the process of taking a physical substance and implanting it into its natural counterpart. We plant the physical substance of a seed into its natural environment, the soil, so that it can grow and flourish. Similar to the seed of man implanted into its natural counterpart, the ovary (egg) of a woman creates a baby. Whether its money deposited in its natural counterpart, such as a bank, or a half-grown tree planted in the dirt, each substance has its natural counterpart or environment that allows it to grow and mature. If you sow any material into an environment that is not its God-ordained natural counterpart, it will not grow, develop, or mature. It is the maturing of what you sow that will bring you a return of a greater substance.

Consider what the bible says about the physical substance we sow into their natural counterpart. *Genesis 4:1 "The man knew Eve his wife. She conceived, and gave birth to Cain, and said, "I have gotten a man with Yahweh's help."* Notice that even though the sexual act was between the husband, Adam, and his wife, Eve, she acknowledged God's help. After getting pregnant, she had to take care of herself, and Adam had to take care of her, for she was the natural environment of his growing seed. After 9 months of development, the child would be born into a new environment suitable for new growth and development.

Genesis 47:23 reads, *"Then Joseph said to the people, 'Behold, I have bought you and your land today for Pharaoh. Behold, here is seed for you, and you shall sow the land."* The people were in the second year of a seven-year famine when they had to sell their land and their services to Pharaoh, who, at Joseph's counsel, had stored up 20% of his grain over the previous seven years. Joseph still expected the farmers to sow seed despite the famine. They sowed because it is the natural environment for the seed. Even in bad conditions, planting is necessary, or there won't be enough for the future. Seasons of failure can be the best time to sow seeds of success. Joseph's anticipation of Egypt's impending famine ultimately led to his success. Joseph struck a deal with the farmers, allowing them to keep 80% of the harvest for their own use and give 20% to Pharaoh. *Genesis 47:24 It will happen at the harvests, that you shall give a fifth to Pharaoh, and four parts will be your own, for seed of the field, for your food, for them of your households, and for food for your little ones.* As stewards, we must find a way to live without depleting our harvest by consuming it all. Previously, they relied entirely on the harvest and didn't store enough to get them through the famine. Now they had to learn to live off the 80% they would have after giving Pharaoh his fifth of the harvest. This precedent is essential when we discuss living by the 80/20 rule later.

Another example of introducing a substance into its natural environment is the way money functions in the economy. *Luke 19:23 reads, "Then why didn't you deposit my money in the bank, and at my coming, I might have earned interest on it?"* The master in the parable did not live off 100% of his earnings; he expected to earn more from what he had not spent. He was financing his lifestyle for his future and his family's. His minimum investment was to have interest earned with a banker. Profitable ventures and interest-earning organizations are the natural environment for growing your money. He wasn't just looking for a storage place for his money; he was betting on people whose ventures his money could help, and he would earn a greater portion of what he invested in return.

SOWING AN ACTION

Actions can be imputed or sewn into their own social environment. The things we do or don't do impact the lives of ourselves and those around us. If we sow actions like attending college, we reap the benefits of an educated mind and the potential opportunities it may open up for us. If we sow actions, such as being there for our children and the children of others, we will see them grow into more confident and productive citizens. Proverbs 22:6 rightly says, *"Train up a child in the way he should go, and when he is old he will not depart from it."* Training is about knowing what works. Guide your child's gifts, temperaments, and the responsibilities given to them for their growth and good. Not living our lives to finish the dreams we never made, but one where they are living their own.

Sowing good actions responsibly often leads to a good return. Isaiah 3:10 reads, *"Tell the righteous that it will be well with them, for they will eat the fruit of their deeds."* Doing good is its own reward, but that doesn't mean that the Lord won't also reward with more. Remember that we are operating under the law of reciprocity. Our good deeds come back in the **MOVE** (*Memories, Opportunities, Victories, Encouragements*) of yourself and those of others. Doing good gives, us greater satisfaction, and people will remember us well. You will find yourself with open doors and doors of opportunity opening up for others. When we do the right things, we are part of every victory around us, and people will encourage us as we encourage them. Titus 3:14 encourages us this way by saying, *"Let our people also learn to maintain good works to meet necessary needs, that they may not be unfruitful.*

One of the most significant problems in our society is that many of the actions people take harm others, leading to distrust and disunity. Bad actions are contrary to loving our neighbors, and if you keep giving, you will get it in return. Job 4:8 reads, *"According to what I have seen, those who plow iniquity and sow trouble, reap the same."* Sowing disorder only brings a harvest of pain, misery, and sin. Sometimes the enemy is in-a-me. That's our sinful nature. **SIN (Self-Indulgent Nature)** is doing what we want and not what the Lord wants. It is rooted in us growing like a super weed. However, like every plant in its natural environment, we uproot sin using the tools and methods given to us by God.

SOWING A THOUGHT

Thoughts can be among the most beneficial or dangerous seeds to sow. Thoughts affect our spiritual views and beliefs. Hosea 10:12 reads, *"Sow to yourselves in righteousness, reap according to kindness. Break up your fallow ground, for it is time to seek Yahweh, until he comes and rains righteousness on you."* The thoughts we meditate on are sowing to ourselves. Minds are the natural environment for thoughts, innovations, ideas, and suggestions. We receive them through learning and experience. Thoughts are spread (sown) through conversations, books, media, music, and anything that affects the five senses of touch, taste, smell, hearing, and sight, causing us to form an opinion about what we have experienced.

What people think is significantly impacted by what they listen to and accept. Hosea 8:7 wasn't kidding when it said some people sow the wind and reap the whirlwind. Sown thoughts establish systems of beliefs that affect not only the individual but also the entire society. If enough people share the same system of beliefs, it has a spiritual impact on how our world functions. Our thought life is the realm where Satan operates. The word devil comes from the Greek Diablo, meaning one who sows thoughts or accuses. John 13:2 reads *"During supper, the devil having already put into the heart of Judas Iscariot, Simon's son, to betray him."* Satan works by sowing thoughts and setting up a system of beliefs that are contrary to God's design. One such system of beliefs asserts that one person is inherently better than another (prejudice). It is this system that led to slavery in Europe and the Americas. This system led to segregation, the underclassing of women, mistreatment of migrant farm workers, apartheid, beatings, attacks on foreigners, and a host of other abuses we should oppose.

> *Galatians 6:9 Let's not be weary in doing good, for we will reap in due season if we don't give up.*

By sowing good seed in a good environment, the steward will do well and please his Lord. This verse tells us that we are never to lose heart or give up sowing. If we, as stewards of God, refuse to give up, we will reap a harvest for our Lord.

REAPING

> *Revelation 14:15 Another angel came out of the temple, crying with a loud voice to him who sat on the cloud, "Send your sickle and reap, for the hour to reap has come; for the harvest of the earth is ripe!"*

Everyone who sows wants to reap. In fact, the purpose of sowing happens to be reaping. Let us define what we mean by reaping. Reaping is the process of gathering the mature fruit of previously sown seed to prepare, save, or use for God's kingdom. Remember, sowing is God's method of redistributing His resources as He desires. Reaping is God's method of replenishing what we previously sown. One problem with reaping is that many people don't know how to do it. Christian leaders often teach people how to sow but rarely instruct people on how to reap. Let's change that right now.

THE REAPER

The **REAPER (Resource Extraction Assistance Person Expecting Rewards)** does not own the harvest. Instead, reapers are dayworkers and laborers sent out into the field. But just like any workman, the reaper receives the benefit of everything harvested. The bigger and better the harvest, the longer the reaper will gather. *John 4:36 says "He who reaps receives wages and gathers fruit to eternal life, that both he who sows and he who reaps may rejoice together.".* As Stewards of God, we are drawing wages from a crop that lasts unto eternal life. As believers, we often don't realize that the grace and finances we draw on are only a small glimpse of what we have reaped in the spiritual realm. We store our treasures in heaven. What we receive on earth is only a small advance on the work we have done.

PLANTING SEED

Let me make something very clear now: "Money is not Seed". Yes, that is true; money is not a seed, but its use operates by the same principle as things reproducing after their own kind. In Genesis 1:28, God commanded humanity to be "fruitful and multiply, fill the earth and subdue it." Whenever we operate with anything in a fruitful manner, it will multiply. Don't be fooled, only living things can reproduce on their own. Money isn't living. It does not have a seed inside itself. What makes money reproduce is the steward who uses God's resources generously and wisely.

What makes money productive is a prudent steward who invests it in fertile ground (a productive environment).

FERTILE GROUND

The power to reap a harvest from what you sow is not dependent on what you have to sow but instead on the fertility of the ministry, business, project, or business venture that you sow into. As stewards, we must be wise in how we allocate God's resources. In 1 Corinthians 3:6, Paul states, "I planted. Apollos watered. But God gave the increase." The seed which Paul planted was the gospel. Apollos watered the seed through care and instruction in the Christian life, but growth comes only through God. The reason it is essential to plant in fertile ground is that it is where God will cause the increase.

> *Isaiah 28:24-26 Does he who plows to sow plow continually? Does he keep turning the soil and breaking the clods? When he has leveled its surface, doesn't he plant the dill, and scatter the cumin seed, and put in the wheat in rows, the barley in the appointed place, and the spelt in its place? For his God instructs him in right judgment and teaches him.*

TILLING THE HARD GROUND

As stewards of God, we should have a clear understanding of what we are investing in God's resources, but that is not always the case. Sometimes, God will have us plant seeds into what appears to be unfertile ground, but He will till the ground and bring life into what seemed dead. When a farmer is ready to plant seeds, if the soil is hard, they will till the ground to prepare it for planting. Untilled ground will not accept seed. Instead, the birds will eat the seed sitting on top of the hard soil. Successful ventures require a solid foundation to thrive. If the foundational work isn't complete, then everything thereafter will fall apart. There must be a clear vision or blueprint for any endeavor to succeed. The working of this vision is how we till the ground.

FERTILIZING

Due to the effects of planting and harsh weather over a season, the ground loses essential nutrients beneficial to plants, requiring fertilization to maintain healthy soil. Fertilizer stinks, but it is a necessary component of the job. Fertilization begins at tilling but is repeated as needed, depending on seed growth. Fertilizing is a necessary part of the job that we dislike doing. It's dirty, it stinks, and you want to get through it quickly, but it enriches the soil, so you get a good harvest.

WATERING THE SOIL

By watering the soil, I mean that it takes work to make anything productive. Deuteronomy 11:10-11 says *"For the land, where you go in to possess isn't like the land of Egypt that you came out of, where you sowed your seed and watered it with your foot, as a garden of herbs; 11but the land that you go over to possess is a land of hills and valleys which drinks water from the rain of the sky"*. Egypt had an irrigation system that sectioned crops into quadrants, with river water running through pathways that the gardener would block with their foot to direct water to a specific section. They watered each section by creating a dam with their foot until the task was complete. However, the promised land was unprepared, and it would be hard work to transport water from a distant source, filling pots with irrigation holes as you walked to water the land. As Stewards, we work hard at what we do, but we do have the promise that as God moves us to a bigger land, the work will become easier and we will have more help.

UPROOTING WEEDS

To keep the land as productive as possible as stewards, we must meet challenges as they arise. A weed is a plant that is undesirable or detrimental to a harvest. Weeds will grow, and in other words, problems will come. Matthew 13:27-28 says, *"The servants of the householder came and said to him, 'Sir, didn't you sow good seed in your field? Where did these darnel weeds come from?' 28"He said to them, 'An enemy has done this.' "The servants asked him, 'Do you want us to go and gather them up?"* When weeds grow, they begin competing with the new plant for nutrients and water in the soil. If the Steward lets these weeds fester, they will grow up and choke the life out of your harvest. Unresolved problems will halt all growth and rob you of your ability to thrive. It is not enough to just cut the weed so it is not visible. That's what happens when you shuffle a problem person to a new department, causing the weeds' roots to grow bigger and stronger underground. No, the weed needs to be dug up by the roots so it will not come back bigger and stronger.

> *Jeremiah 5:24 They don't say in their heart, 'Let's now fear Yahweh our God, who gives rain, both the former and the latter, in its season, who preserves to us the appointed weeks of the harvest.*

HARVEST

Harvest is a season when the steward works the hardest, as there is a lot of work to do and a limited amount of time to complete it. Some people pray to the Lord for a harvest, but when it comes, they miss it because they aren't working hard. They treat harvesting time as if it were a storage season, where everything is already in the bank. **HARVEST (Having A Renewable Valuable Earn Something Terrific)** is the season when what you have sown has grown and matured to the point it is ready to be reaped. One of the most important things you can know about reaping is that it takes some time for your seed to mature to the point where the steward can draw the most significant benefit from it. If you try to reap before the season of Harvest, you will have much less for your efforts. In many business ventures, the Harvest may be plain for all to see. New customers and business contracts are necessary for the effort to expand, but the path to reaping a spiritual harvest may not be clear. The steward needs to pray and ask the Master of the Harvest for the latter rains.

STORING UP

Once you have gathered the harvest, it is broken into portions and assigned to its purpose. The more you have, the more people will ask for it. I am very clear with others that all my money is assigned. Allocate your money for living expenses, charitable giving, savings, investments, or personal enjoyment. Don't loan out money that is assigned or allocated to a purpose. If you still have money left over after allocating your funds, then you can consider lending it to a trustworthy person. The Israelites stored grain by pressing it into the container, then moving it around so the grain would be displaced closer together, allowing more grain to pour in. In the same way, you control the flow of your blessing.

KNOWING YOUR SEASON

Ecclesiastes 3:1-3 For everything there is a season, and a time for every purpose under heaven: a time to be born, and a time to die; a time to plant, and a time to pluck up that which is planted; a time to kill, and a time to heal; a time to break down, and a time to build up;

There are certain times and seasons in every steward's life. A good steward recognizes the **SEASON (Shifting Environment Analyzed State Of Nature)** they are in and prepares accordingly. Sometimes, the reason we struggle with our finances is that we wasted extra resources when we had them. The following are some of the seasons of stewardship you can expect to see.

- Sowing – In this season, the Steward needs to spread as much seed as they possibly can into any ground God has blessed.
- Laboring – In this season, the Steward works to build the ministry or business venture they have sown into.
- Watering – This is a season of prayer and fasting. Where you pray for the blessing on the venture, for people, and for your personal needs
- Reaping – This is a time of spiritual, emotional, psychological, social, physical, or financial blessing.
- Abundance – This is a time of storing some away in preparation for the future. It is not good for the steward to become wasteful with resources.
- Famine – This is a lean season marked by hardships, financial woes, and troubles. The steward draws steadily but slowly from the stored resources.

SEASONS OF A STEWARD

Like most stewards, we are continuously sowing seed. Because the sowing of seed is constant, we can expect to be in at least the first three seasons sowing, laboring, and watering if not more seasons, at all times. You may be watering in one area while you're reaping in another. Sometimes we reap for business, other times for our spiritual walk or family relationships. God is always working on one or more areas of your life, even if it's not the one you want. For those who consistently sow, the potential to reap at a moment's notice is always present. That is why stewards who sow and sow and sow have the confidence that whenever they get into a spiritual, emotional, or financial crisis, God will bring them out. They have deposited so much that when they call on the name of Jesus, He immediately opens the floodgates of heaven to pour them out a blessing that they can't even handle.

STOCK MARKET SEASONS

Stock market seasons are historical trends driven by specific events, investor behavior, and consumer shopping habits. They are not guarantees, but predictable patterns that form economic cycles, acting as seasons. I am not a financial adviser or a day trader. I live in the USA, so I base the **STOCK (Shares Traded Of Company Kept)** season on the US market. Seasonality is informative, but it should not be the sole factor in affecting trade decisions. Events in the news, inflation, interest rates, trade agreements, manufacturing trends, severe weather patterns, and other factors influence stock market seasons. The US market has generally performed well, with the S&P 500 and Nasdaq being the biggest winners, typically achieving gains of around 9 to 15% over the past 20 years.

STOCK SEASON CHART

· · · · ·

January	Stocks rise related to tax-related selling in December.
February	After the January barometer, February can be a cool-down month that predicts trends.
March	Usually, it's a good month for stocks.
April	Tax season ends, and payouts are typically received, leading to increased spending and investing by individual consumers.
May	The May selloff occurs amid investor anticipation of weaker summer results, potentially leading to a rebound in the fall.
June	Beginning of the summer slump. Travel and leisure industries tend to perform better.
July	During the summer slump, July sometimes rallies
August	The summer slump is in full effect as vacationing & summer school closures lead to less investing.
September	A net negative month continues—typically a bearish close of the third quarter, which leads to a rebalancing of funds.
October	Fall reinvestment of funds after the summertime slump in trading
November	Growth can occur just before the US Thanksgiving and remain strong until Christmas.
December	Increased holiday sales affect fourth-quarter profits, as prices rise in anticipation of the new year.

Scan to watch video: Healthy Seasons

CHAPTER FIVE

GIVING IT AWAY AND GETTING IT BACK

· · · · · · · · · · · ·

2 CORINTHIANS 9:6

Remember this: he who sows sparingly will also reap sparingly. He who sows bountifully will also reap bountifully.

BACK TO RECIPROCITY

The point made in this verse is that you can only get back what you put in. The more you put in, the more you have to take out, much as when you deposit money in a bank. Opportunities will ultimately present themselves if you put more time, energy, and money into your pursuits. It is crucial to emphasize that a steward is a manager, not an owner, of their Master's property. God expects His stewards to operate with the same kind of heart that He has. In business, employees need to understand their company's vision and culture so they can operate within it. God's stewards need to operate with His vision and heart. The steward who has learned the Heart of God, generosity, and joy will be present.

GIVING GENEROUSLY

Generous giving stems from the stewards' recognition that they are not the owners, and their realization in their hearts to do good. In giving, it is the steward's responsibility to sow what is not his. Even the seed belongs to the LORD. In sowing seed, the sower is never to become attached to the seed. Part of the problem we have in giving is that we have become so attached to our finances that we want to hoard them or use them for our desires. Instead of scattering seeds, we hold on to them. The sower who keeps a clenched fist on his goods will sow very sparingly and therefore not reap a harvest. Selfishness and hoarding hinder the flow of blessings that come from being a generous steward. Generosity opens up a river of blessings for the believer.

THE BLESSEDNESS OF GIVING

Acts 20:35 In all things I gave you an example, that so laboring you ought to help the weak, and to remember the words of the Lord Jesus, that he himself said, 'It is more blessed to give than to receive.'

The bible says it is more blessed to give than receive. There are many different reasons for this. The first point is that if you have something to give, then you have already received it. Acts 11:29 says, *"And to the extent that any of the disciples had means, each of them determined to send a contribution for the relief of the brothers and sisters living in Judea (NASB)."* We give from the surplus, not scarcity. Surplus giving doesn't mean that those struggling should not give. Having been raised in poverty, I've seen many who have little provide for those who have nothing. However, your first responsibility is to care for your own home before caring for someone else's. Those with a surplus have a greater responsibility because they are experiencing the promises of God. *Deuteronomy 28:12 The LORD will open for you His good storehouse, the heavens, to give rain to your land in its season and to bless every work of your hand; and you will lend to many nations, but you will not borrow.* Those operating in the promise have the heavens open to them. We want to reach a point where God blesses every work of our hands. Those operating in the blessing are to be the lenders, not borrowers. We must be careful when dealing with borrowers, as many people are already struggling due to poor financial habits. Trusting someone with a bad track record is unwise. Giving to them is like gambling. You should only give what you can afford to lose.

Luke 6:30-31 speaks of what we call the royal law, saying, *"Give to everyone who asks of you, and whoever takes away what is yours, do not demand it back. Treat people the same way you want them to treat you."* It is our third reason: helping others in the way we would want to receive help if we were in their shoes. Empathetic giving is the law of our divine king, whose heart yearns to help those in need. Our final reason for being givers is that it demonstrates our growth. We call the pocket book the final frontier because it's the last thing most people want to give up. When the rich young ruler approached Jesus, he was missing one thing. *"Jesus said to him, If you wish to be perfect, go, sell what you have and give to the poor, and you will have treasure in heaven. Then come, follow me"* (Matthew 19:21). Sometimes we give and get an instant return; other times we store up treasures in heaven. Money may not be your thing, but God calls us all to give up something to follow Him. When we give what is precious to God, He becomes our treasure and ensures we have His presence and protection.

GROWING IN GIVING

Psalms 112:5 It is well with the man who deals graciously and lends. He will maintain his cause in judgment.

The steward should be developing their abilities to manage resources, including their giving. If you begrudge giving, you won't get much out of it. It is vital to put our faith, hope, and love into our giving. Our **FAITH (Forsaking All I Trust Him)** moves us to do good and connects our relationship with God to our giving. Our hope inspires us to be content with what we have and to be more attached to God than to material things. Love places our hearts in the proper position to not only do the right thing but do it in the right way. You may have worked for it, but remember it was God who caused the increase. To grow in their giving, the steward needs to understand that giving is as much an art as it is a science, and a gift.

THE ART OF GIVING

Giving is an art in that the more you give, the better you become at giving. Just like any other skill or ability, the more you exercise it, the more proficient you become. Sowing seed becomes like delivering newspapers. When riding a bike and delivering papers, you must develop your arm and your aim. In the beginning, some papers end up in the bushes, others in the fountain, and you may hit a window or two. As time passes, your ability to deliver the paper and toss it directly on the porch becomes easier. Initially, giving was a strenuous exercise for most of us. We started giving a little, then gradually increased our level of giving. Challenging ourselves at each place of growth in giving. Through experience, we learn to sow by giving. Givers give, and the more they give, the better a giver they become.

THE SCIENCE OF GIVING

There are five basic types of science. They include the natural sciences, such as biology, and the physical sciences, like chemistry; the applied sciences, such as engineering; the more formal sciences, such as logic; and the social sciences, such as economics. Giving is a part of the economics of science, as all Christian giving is to be governed by the law of God. The Holy

Scriptures outline the principles that guide Christian giving and steward-ship. Our giving is regulated in a sense to accomplish God's purposes in this world. We give not just out of need, but out of purpose, so spreading the gospel and fostering Christian growth is not optional. However, our giving should be intelligent and intentional. If a charity spends 80% of its money on salaries and fundraising, it isn't very effective. Check their charity rating to see whether they handle the funds you give them responsibly.

In the science of giving, intelligent giving stops toxic charity. Toxic charity fosters dependence, not development. An adage says, "Give a man a fish, you feed him for a day, teach him how to fish, and you feed him for a lifetime. Giving for an immediate need should be generous, but with the purpose of not sustaining the need. Feeding a starving nation has led some nations not to develop their agricultural sectors. Farmers who could not compete with the price of free food went out of business. Instead of developing their education and agriculture, those nations invested in de-fense spending, leaving them to rely on continued foreign aid to feed their people. That's toxic. Food giveaways are an effective way to meet immedi-ate needs. Still, a cooperative food-sharing network that purchases in bulk and allows people experiencing poverty to buy food at a lower cost while maintaining their dignity is a better long-term solution.

THE GIFT OF GIVING

Romans 12: 6-8 Having gifts differing according to the grace that was given to us: if prophecy, let's prophesy according to the proportion of our faith; or service, let's give ourselves to service; or he who teaches, to his teaching; or he who exhorts, to his exhorting; he who gives, let him do it with generosity; he who rules, with diligence; he who shows mercy, with cheerfulness.

Spiritual gifts such as prophecy, faith, teaching, and giving come from God. God has endowed certain believers with the ability to be totally unselfish, giving of themselves and their resources. Giving without seeking anything in return seems to be their natural response to the world. Whenever they see a need, they fulfill it. Not all believers possess the **GIFT (Grace Is Freely Transferred)** of giving, but all have a responsibility to give. Even if the steward does not have a God-given inclination to give through the art and science of giving, they can still be a blessed giver.

3 TYPES OF GIVING

The bible gives us instructions on giving. There are three general types of giving listed in the Bible: relational covenant giving, which involves the tithe; replacement giving, often called alms, which derives from the Greek word for pity or mercy; and redemptive offerings.

RELATIONAL COVENANT GIVING

> Genesis 28:20-22 *"Jacob vowed a vow, saying, "If God will be with me, and will keep me in this way that I go, and will give me bread to eat, and clothing to put on, so that I come again to my father's house in peace, and Yahweh will be my God, then this stone, which I have set up for a pillar, will be God's house. Of all that you will give me I will surely give a tenth to you."*

Tithing is giving based on a covenant. Tithing is a covenant or required giving that affirms Jehovah as our God. Jehovah is an English translation of God's Hebrew covenant name, Yahweh, transliterated through the Greek and then Latin languages. God revealed Himself as the God of Abraham and Isaac, but did not mention being the God of Jacob (Genesis 28:13). This would change. Jacob committed to a journey with God. His promise stated that if he made it back to where he was running from, Jehovah would also be Jacob's God. During this time, Jacob established a relationship with God built on commitment and eventually came to give Him a tenth of all he had. Most scholars argue that, since there was no biblical priesthood at that time, Jacob would give the tithe through service and sacrifice. Some suggest that Jacob might have fulfilled his vow by giving it to Esau, whom he had tricked and cheated. Genesis 32:13-15 *"He lodged there that night, and took from that which he had with him, a present for Esau, his brother: two hundred female goats and twenty male goats, two hundred ewes and twenty rams, thirty milk camels and their colts, forty cows, ten bulls, twenty female donkeys and ten foals."* Since giving is done in silence, we don't know if this is how Jacob fulfilled his vow. We do know that the Edomites, who were Esau's descendants, worshiped Jehovah for some time before turning to other gods, making this a possibility. Still, where the Bible is silent, we should also remain silent.

The Bible describes what we are to tithe in Leviticus 27:30-32, which reads, *"All the tithe of the land, whether of the seed of the land or of the fruit of the trees, is Yahweh's. It is holy to Yahweh. If a man redeems anything of his tithe, he shall add a fifth part to it. All the tithe of the herds or the flocks, whatever passes under the rod, the tenth shall be holy to Yahweh."* The Israelites were to give what grows, whether it grows from the land or it grows from within the flock. The word tithing means tenth, and a tenth of all that they had belonged to God. The Israelites tithed flocks and crops, not money. An individual might want to keep certain animals to grow the herd through mating or to ensure sufficient food supplies. In this case, they added a fifth to the tithe's value and gave money instead.

REPLACEMENT GIVING OF ALMS

> *Matthew 25:37-40 "Then the righteous will answer him, saying, 'Lord, when did we see you hungry, and feed you; or thirsty, and give you a drink? When did we see you as a stranger, and take you in; or naked, and clothe you? When did we see you sick, or in prison, and come to you?' "The King will answer them, 'Most certainly I tell you, inasmuch as you did it to one of the least of these my brothers, you did it to me.'*

There are several reasons why we refer to alms as replacement giving. The first is that it replaces what the individual has lost or lacks. **ALMS (Affectionate Love Makes Sacrifice)** giving is the giving of mercy in a tangible form. It meets the individual's need, providing them with a moment of security so that God can minister to their soul. The second reason is that Jesus says that when you do it for them, you have done it to Him. Christ places Himself in the position of need with those whom we help. The righteous answered this way because they didn't realize that when they helped those in need, they were actually helping Christ. His position replaced their poverty. The third reason alms are called replacement giving is that God rewards them. Proverbs 19:17 reads, *"He who has pity on the poor lends to Yahweh; he will reward him."* You can take that to the bank. God will replace what you've used. Sometimes, He answers you financially, but other times, He rewards us with peace, protection, and His presence.

As mentioned earlier, almsgiving is an act that demonstrates God's mercy and care for a suffering world. Not all those in need are poor; they are just in need. Proverbs 17:5 says, *"Whoever mocks the poor reproaches his Maker. He who is glad at calamity shall not be unpunished."* God sees need and poverty as an opportunity for mercy and doesn't take them lightly. **POVERTY (Position Of Victimizing Economic Restrictions Threatening You)** places people at jeopardy, and a few bad turns could threaten anybody. When we give to someone in need, we do so to help them. God looks at people in need and sees them as if He were in need.

In reality, people who have very little often have more faith than those who have a lot. That's why James 2:5 says, *"Listen, my beloved brethren: Has God not chosen the poor of this world to be rich in faith and heirs of the kingdom which He promised to those who love Him?"* Those suffering financial insecurity often have spiritual stability because they have no options but to trust in God. The church is to be a support system, helping them with their needs.

OFFERINGS (REDEMPTIVE) GIVING

Exodus 25:1-2 Yahweh spoke to Moses, saying, "Speak to the children of Israel, that they take an offering for me. From everyone whose heart makes him willing you shall take my offering."

Offerings are voluntary giving. Unlike tithes, the Israelites did not give offerings out of obligation. Instead, they gave offerings out of their love and deep respect for God. There were many types of offerings listed in the Old Testament (Heave offerings, wave offerings, burnt offerings, peace offerings, sin offerings, drink offerings). All of these offerings had a redemptive purpose. Genesis 22:13-14 reads *"Abraham lifted up his eyes, and looked, and saw that behind him was a ram caught in the thicket by his horns. Abraham went and took the ram, and offered him up for a burnt offering instead of his son. Abraham called the name of that place Yahweh Will Provide. As it is said to this day, "On Yahweh's mountain, it will be provided."* Offerings are given freely and always redeem the person, relationship, family, or nation.

Redemption deals with reconnecting, restoring, resanctifying, reconciling, restitution, repairing, and recommitting. Exodus 29:36 states, *"Every day you shall offer the bull of sin offering for atonement: and you shall cleanse the altar, when you make atonement for it; and you shall anoint it, to sanctify it."* The sacrifice made atonement for both the individual and the altar. When there was a fault, flaw, or failure, the redemptive power of the offering took care of it. Redemption requires the person to get right, for we see in Leviticus 5:5-6 *"It shall be, when he is guilty of one of these, he shall confess that in which he has sinned: and he shall bring his trespass offering to Yahweh for his sin which he has sinned, a female from the flock, a lamb or a goat, for a sin offering; and the priest shall make atonement for him concerning his sin."* Confession cancels confusion, but it's not a proposition of either confession or sacrifice. It is a both/and proposition. We confess our wrongdoings and make sacrifices, demonstrating the importance of redemption to us.

CHEERFUL GIVING

> *2 Corinthians 9:7 Let each man give according as he has determined in his heart; not grudgingly, or under compulsion; for God loves a cheerful giver.*

The Bible says that God doesn't look at outward appearances, but at the heart. We focus so much on the amount that we often forget the heart of it. Looking at amounts is looking at the external, but the joy in giving is what God loves. Giving includes acts of kindness, mercy, love, and faithfulness. There is a lot more that we can give than just money, so everyone has something they can give. Joyful giving is when people who profess to love Him act in accordance with that love. The receiver has a momentary thrill of getting, but still has worries. The giver has an enduring joy from what they give. In this way, both the giver and receiver are blessed. Generosity with joy comes from the love we have for God and rests on the faith we have in Him.

For some people, giving is getting rid of what they don't want or need. Others may see it as an obligation, but God looks at it as an exchange. Giving isn't always easy, especially when we fear approaching a lean time and having to cut back on things we desire to do. However, it reflects our faith and faithfulness. When we give in this way, it implies that we understand. We are not attached to things but to God. Remember, giving is God's way of relocating resources to the right places, with the idea that He will restore more to the giver. The steward, happy in the performance of their duties, demonstrates to God that they believe He is a good and loving master, and that they are His willing bond servants.

VERSES ABOUT MONEY THAT DON'T MEAN WHAT YOU THINK

• • • • •

Luke 6:38 Give, and it will be given to you: good measure, pressed down, shaken together, and running over, will be given to you. For with the same measure you measure it will be measured back to you. – The preceding two verses (V.36-37) instruct us to be merciful because God is merciful, not to judge or condemn others, but to set them free so we can be set free. Although this verse is most often used to preach about giving offerings, the context is actually about giving forgiveness to others, and God will multiply the forgiveness you receive in return.

Ecclesiastes 10:19 A feast is made for laughter, and wine makes the life glad; and money is the answer for all things. You may have heard that money answers all things as a reason to support one's needs, but it is a misapplication of the verse. Ecclesiastes chapters 9 and 10 contrast the actions of the wise and the fool. The previous three verses describe how unfortunate it is to have immature leaders who prioritize themselves, feasting for enjoyment, rather than leaders who eat to gain strength and work. It leaves conditions in need of repair, and the need for more money is often seen as the solution to everything. So, for the fool, the need for money is the answer to all things; the wise answer by getting to work.

Matthew 19:21 Jesus said to him, "If you want to be perfect, go, sell what you have, and give to the poor, and you will have treasure in heaven; and come, follow me – This verse has led many to give up their possessions and take a vow of poverty as a discipline to following Jesus. However, the focus isn't on possessions but on what possesses you. Jesus is asking us to let go of whatever holds us back from fully following Him. For some, it may be money and possessions, for others, it's something different. The verse isn't about possession, but about what is missing in your heart.

Scan to watch video: Kingdom Economics

CHAPTER SIX

THE GOD POCKET KINGDOM

. . . .

GENESIS 14:19-20

He blessed him, and said, "Blessed be Abram of God Most High, possessor of heaven and earth. Blessed be God Most High, who has delivered your enemies into your hand." Abram gave him a tenth of all.

As mentioned previously, Tithing is giving based upon having a covenant. As we see with Abraham, the practice existed before the establishment of the law. Abraham received a blessing from Melchizedek and then gave him a tenth of the spoils as an act of gratitude. Melchizedek was a priest of God before the law, the Levitical priesthood, or even Levi. To understand the tithe, you must first understand the concept of covenant relationships. Covenant relationships typically originate from an agreement or contract. Some say covenants differ from contracts in that contracts are for those who don't trust each other. Covenants are relational and require trust, loyalty, and caring. There are three different types of covenants found in the scriptures.

THE SELF-IMPOSED COVENANT

Genesis 15:17-18 It came to pass that, when the sun went down, and it was dark, behold, a smoking furnace and a flaming torch passed between these pieces. In that day Yahweh made a covenant with Abram, saying, "I have given this land to your offspring, from the river of Egypt to the great river, the river Euphrates."

A self-imposed covenant is a **COVENANT (Commitment Of Vows Ensuring New Alliances Necessary Tasks)** where one obligates oneself for the benefit of another. In Genesis 15, God establishes a blood covenant with Abraham, where two individuals would normally walk through pieces of cut-up animals to proclaim that if either broke the covenant, what happened to the animals would happen to the violator. However, before walking through the pieces together, a deep sleep fell upon Abraham (Genesis 15:12). As seen above, God walked through the pieces in Himself in two manifestations. The Lord walking alone signified that God would die regardless of which party broke the covenant. The sign of a blood covenant is death. Death initiated it, and death would be the consequence if one broke it. God could not break a covenant He made, but He self-imposed a covenant term that He would also be the one to die if Abraham's descendants were to break the covenant. Considering that Jesus stood in as Abraham's representative, manifesting either as the smoking pot or the flaming torch, the self-imposed terms meant that if Abraham's descendants broke the covenant, He would die in their place. The death would end the broken covenant and establish a new covenant in His blood.

THE OTHER IMPOSED COVENANT

> *Genesis 6:18 But I will establish my covenant with you. You shall come into the ship, you, your sons, your wife, and your sons' wives with you.*

An other-imposed covenant is one in which someone imposes an obligation on another, often with little or no benefit to themselves or to the individual on whom they impose it. The terms are set solely by the one imposing the covenant without outside input. There is no bargaining. You can take it or leave it. God established a positive covenant of life with Noah to preserve his family from a great disaster. Nothing in this covenant depended on human actions, and everyone outside the covenant would perish. The promise of the covenant was so powerful that God set a sign of the bow in the clouds after the rain, ensuring that He would never use this destructive method of a flood globally again.

THE MUTUAL COVENANT

> *Genesis 17:7-8 I will establish my covenant between me and you and your offspring after you throughout their generations for an everlasting covenant, to be a God to you and to your offspring after you. I will give to you, and to your offspring after you, the land where you are traveling, all the land of Canaan, for an everlasting possession. I will be their God."*

A mutual covenant is a contract in which both parties have mutual obligations and mutual benefits. Here we have the covenant of circumcision (Genesis 17:10-12). The cutting away of the flesh would be a sign of the covenant. Abraham commanded that all males in his house and all his descendants would be circumcised, and God established a covenant to be their God. Abraham's decision to circumcise his household reveals that he wanted this covenant just as much as God did. In a sense, this was a covenant of cutting away so we could fit together. We see this in marriages where the couple leaves their parents to cleave to their spouse. The mutual covenant contains agreed-upon terms and conditions that we must adhere to, regardless of our preferences.

ELEMENTS OF A COVENANT

We identify specific elements or portions within a covenant. Covenants generally begin with a preamble that identifies the parties involved. Then, it provides a historical note on the parties past relationships. Next are the shared or imposed stipulations that must be adhered to to maintain the covenant. Biblical covenants have signs as memorials, rather than signatures, to serve as witnesses to the stipulations of the covenant. Circumcision, the rainbow, and the blood of the New Covenant in eucharistic communion are all signs of the covenant they represent. It is also customary to have a list of witnesses made to confirm the covenant. We see this repeatedly in Deuteronomy (4:26, 30:19, 31:28), where heaven and earth are called witnesses to the covenant of the law, which Jesus referred to in Matthew 24:35, saying, *"Heaven and earth will pass away, but my words will not pass away."* The final aspect of a covenant is a listing of the blessings received from being faithful and the curses that occur if one breaks the covenant.

Tithing is a mutually imposed, mutually obligated covenant. God is obligated to be our God, and we are obligated to be His people. The Suzerain treaties of the medieval serfdom era offer us a glimpse of the covenant relationship we have with God. In the suzerain treaties, the serfdom, which was a small kingdom run by a steward, would become a vassal state of the larger kingdom. The smaller kingdom would act as a

Steward overseeing a portion of the larger kingdom. The larger kingdom would provide property to bless the steward, protect them from other kingdoms, and settle disputes through intervention. The smaller kingdom, run by a steward, would fight alongside other vassal states when needed, remain obedient to the king, and regularly pay tribute from what they gained.

The tithe is a tribute given by the steward of God's resources to **HONOR (Having Officially Noticed Our Respect)** the covenant relationship they have. We see several cases where kings were obligated to give to someone in a higher position. Many times, this was involuntary. One story that illustrates the concept of tribute to the king is in the parable of the talents in Luke 19. A man goes away to receive a kingdom and gives one servant ten talents, another five talents, and the last one talent, each according to the ability they had already demonstrated to him. Luke 19:17 records Jesus speaking of the one whom the master gave ten talents and had gained ten more. "He said to him, "*Well done, you good servant! Because you were found faithful with very little, you shall have authority over ten cities.*" The one who gained ten became a vassal ruler over a large area containing ten cities. The one who gained five talents became the ruler of a region of five cities. The one who hid the talent, giving no increase, received only condemnation. He could have done more, but chose to do nothing. Let's see what the scriptures say about tribute.

God desires His Tribute - Malachi 1:6 "A son honors his father, and a servant his master. If I am a father, then where is my honor? And if I am a master, where is the respect due me?" says Yahweh of Armies to you priests who despise my name. "You say, 'How have we despised your name?'

Kings Paid Tribute to Other Kings - 2 Kings 18:14-15 Hezekiah king of Judah sent to the king of Assyria at Lachish, saying, "I have offended you. Withdraw from me. That which you put on me, I will bear." The king of Assyria appointed to Hezekiah king of Judah three hundred talents of silver and thirty talents of gold.

Nations Forced to Pay Tribute Rebelled ~ Genesis 14:4 They served Chedorlaomer for twelve years, and in the thirteenth year they rebelled.

The Defeated were Placed under Tribute ~ Judges 1:28 And it came to pass, when Israel was strong, that they put the Canaanites under tribute, but did not completely drive them out.

TITHING AS A SYSTEM OF TAXATION

Malachi 3:10 Bring the whole tithe into the storehouse, that there may be food in my house, and test me now in this," says Yahweh of Armies, "if I will not open you the windows of heaven, and pour you out a blessing, that there will not be enough room for.

As mentioned, when the king was placed under a covenant by a stronger king, the lesser king was required to pay a set tribute that the stronger king imposed on him. The Hebrew word "Ma`aser," translated as "tithe," means one-tenth, and God set His tribute at one-tenth. Like taxation, we take the one-tenth tribute from the increase of what we have made. The tithe is one-tenth of income earnings. If you are employed, you would deduct it from your paycheck, as the entire check is considered the increase. If you run a business, the tithe is calculated from profits after deducting product cost from sales. The **TITHE (Tribute Invested To His Excellency)** became a method of taxation for the strong King (God), who would provide the support the steward needed. When God gave the Old Testament law, there was a marriage of the priesthood and the state. The Judges were the religious and social leaders of their day, backed by the tribal heads, who were local leaders, and the Levites, who were national officials.

That is correct; the Levites were the governing body of Israel, which was a theocracy. Theocracy meant that God ruled Israel, which also meant the Levites were the emissaries of His rule. There was no change in the government system until the people rejected God as their King *in* 1 Samuel 8:6-7, which reads, *"But the thing displeased Samuel when they said, 'Give us a king to judge us." Samuel prayed to Yahweh. Yahweh said to Samuel, "Listen to the voice of the people in all that they tell you; for they have not rejected you, but they have rejected me as the king over them."*

LEVITICAL DUTIES

The Levites' first duty was to serve God. Deuteronomy 10:8 states, *"At that time Yahweh set apart the tribe of Levi to bear the ark of Yahweh's covenant, to stand before Yahweh to minister to him, and to bless in his name, to this day."* Whether it was carrying water for the temple or bearing the ark of the covenant before the people, the **LEVITE (Levi's Entourage's Vocation Is Temple Employee)** primary role was to serve God. However, they also performed many civil functions, such as:

1. The Legal/Judicial System of Israel

> *Deuteronomy 17:9 You shall come to the priests who are Levites and to the judge who shall be in those days. You shall inquire, and they shall give you the verdict."*

When there was a legal dispute, the people went to the Levites, who served as the nation's legal judicial system. The judge refers to the military or prophetic leader chosen by God among the people, with whom the Levites worked. Just as when Moses led Israel, the heaviest cases came to him (Exodus 18:25-26). However, the bulk of cases were handled by those set to judge, which at the time of entering the Promised Land were the Levites.

2. The Religious Worship and Civil Celebrations

> *1 Chronicles 25:6 All these were under the hands of their father for song in Yahweh's house, with cymbals, stringed instruments, and harps, for the service of God's house: Asaph, Jeduthun, and Heman being under the order of the king.*

King David divided the Levitical families with musical abilities into groups that would lead Israel in worship. They were already serving daily at the temple, but this extension led to the handling of civil celebrations and even worshipping God to bring His involvement when the armies of Israel went out to war.

3. The Levites Lead their Educational System

> *2 Chronicles 17:9 They taught in Judah, having the book of Yahweh's law with them. They went about throughout all the cities of Judah and taught among the people.*

Civil and religious instruction came from the Levites. While practical trades were learned through apprenticeship programs, working alongside their parents and families, scholastic education came from the Levites. The Levites served as teachers and instructors, ensuring that the people were familiar with the laws of God. Tradition has it that they even taught basic reading and writing to the youth.

4. Levites Served as Royal Bodyguards

> *2 Chronicles 23:7 The Levites shall surround the king, every man with his weapons in his hand. Whoever comes into the house, let him be slain. Be with the king when he comes in and when he goes out.*

For years, the Levites had a trained policing force at the temple to protect it from trouble. They served as community officers within the court and civil affairs for the people. When called upon, they acted as royal bodyguards, similar to the American Secret Service or the Papal Swiss Guard. They put their lives on the line to protect the king, effectively serving as the national police.

5. Levites Managed the Revenue and Welfare System

> *2 Chronicles 31:14 Kore the son of Imnah the Levite, the gatekeeper at the east gate, was over the free will offerings of God, to distribute Yahweh's offerings and the most holy things.*

The distribution of the gifts given to God was under the care and supervision of the Levites. Whether it was taking care of the temple or running a food program for those in need, all activities were supervised by the Levites. As an American, I would relate this function to Social Security for older adults, the SNAP food program, which assists with food shortage needs, Medical services to meet health needs, and other social assistance programs.

6. The Levites Served as Health and Safety Inspectors

Leviticus 14:36 The priest shall command that they empty the house, before the priest goes in to examine the plague, that all that is in the house not be made unclean. Afterward the priest shall go in to inspect the house.

Whether it was mold in the house or a spot on the leper, the Levites served as the health and safety commission, determining isolation procedures and how to cleanse a property thoroughly before allowing it to be inhabited. They would even inspect homes to ensure they met building standards. Making them both building and health inspectors.

7. The Levites Operated the Transportation and Logistics

Numbers 1:51 When the tabernacle is to move, the Levites shall take it down; and when the tabernacle is to be set up, the Levites shall set it up. The stranger who comes near shall be put to death..

When the Israelites traveled through the wilderness, the Levites packed up the tabernacle and its holy things and moved. The entire nation would follow them at a distance, each in the order given to them. The Levites handled travel and all logistical issues that arose. Moving a crowd that big safely required a lot of planning and help. Levites regulated the transportation of the entire nation.

YES, IT IS A TAX

The tithe is a required giving received by the Levites. We can clearly see that the Levites were the civil and religious government of Israel. They either entirely handled or contributed to every form of government. If we consider the high-ranking government cabinet or department positions in our nation, the Levites were part of all of them. Whether it was military, transportation, education, judicial, health, welfare, or more, the Levites were involved in it all. God doesn't use tribute money (tithes) for Himself; He gives it to the Levites, who form the government, thereby making tithes a form of taxation.

AMOUNT OF THE OLD TESTAMENT TITHE

The word tithe means a tenth. That is why you have heard that to tithe is to give God 10%. Contrary to what you may have heard, the biblical tithe in the Old Testament is not 10% of your income. Yes, I did say that 10% of your yearly income is not the Old Testament Biblical Tithe. Although the word 'tithe' means 10%, the Israelites did not tithe once; instead, they gave tithes or ten percent of their income on three separate occasions for different purposes.

3 TITHES – 20%, 20%, 30%

The first tithe we see in scripture is the tithe that God ordained to provide for ministry. If your church discusses tithing, this is what they mean. Numbers 18:21 records this saying, *"To the children of Levi, behold, I have given all the tithe in Israel for an inheritance, in return for their service which they serve, even the service of the Tent of Meeting."* Tithing provided for the necessary cost of ministry in Israel. Unlike other tribes, the Levites did not receive their own land; instead, they lived in Levitical cities, dispersed among the other tribes of Israel. Deuteronomy 10:9 reads, *"Therefore Levi has no portion nor inheritance with his brothers; Yahweh is his inheritance, according as Yahweh your God spoke to him."* The Levites took care of the things of God so that God would be their inheritance, and because of this, He provided a tenth of the yearly income collected throughout Israel to support them.

Israel gave the second tithe taken in support of celebrations ordained by God each year. This tithe provides for the three mandatory and four non-mandatory feasts that the Israelites were required to observe each year. Deuteronomy 14:23 states, *"You shall eat before Yahweh your God, in the place which he chooses to cause his name to dwell, the tithe of your grain, of your new wine, and of your oil, and the firstborn of your herd and of your flock; that you may learn to fear Yahweh your God always."* The Levites did not receive the second tithe because the Israelites consumed and shared it with others who lacked the resources to participate in the celebrations.

A third tithe was an additional 10% collected every three years to support widows who could not work and resident aliens. The third-year tithe was Israel's welfare system. These were people fleeing slavery or famine in their homeland, as mentioned in the book of Ruth. Deuteronomy 14:28-29 reads, *"At the end of every three years you shall bring all the tithe of your increase in the same year, and shall store it within your gates. The Levite, because he has no portion nor inheritance with you, as well as the foreigner living among you, the fatherless, and the widow who are within your gates shall come, and shall eat and be satisfied; that Yahweh your God may bless you in all the work of your hand which you do".* The storehouse was a large food distribution center designed to care for those in need. History tells us that funding for wars drew upon the storehouse to purchase food and supplies for the troops.

From the three different tithes listed in scripture. The Israelites would give 20% of their income for the first two years and 30% in the third year. Then the 20-20-30 cycle would start over again. Over each 3 years, this would be an average of 23 1/3%. The Historical tithing concept differs significantly from the 10% concept many of us have previously learned. Some churches use tithing to support their ministry, while others do not.

One reason some do not use it is that we are not Levitical priests. Another reason some churches do not use it is that we are not under the law, but rather are under grace. Which really shoots them in the foot when you practice it. Although the arguments are valid, many make them not on theological grounds but because of matters of the heart. The discussion of the church's system of giving can be held in fellowship rather than in parking lots, on phone calls, or on social media posts. Let's discuss some questions about tithing.

> *Malachi 3:11 I will rebuke the devourer for your sakes, and he shall not destroy the fruits of your ground; neither shall your vine cast its fruit before its time in the field," says Yahweh of Armies.*

QUESTIONS ABOUT TITHING

Some may ask, if Tithing is the Old Testament system of taxation, why should I tithe today since I already pay taxes to my government? One reason we do not pay the second and third tithe is that the taxes we pay to the government now fulfill those functions. National holidays and civil welfare are government functions. The first tithe, however, is intended to support the ministry, and God expects the believer to support it. Additionally, Leviticus 27:30-32 instructs us that the tithe is holy to the Lord. Indeed, we no longer live by the Law but by Grace. Tithing sets the base minimum for giving. There is nothing against going over 10% as anything above would be a redemptive offering. Tithing is part of the **LAW (Legal Acts Waged)**. Still, it was initiated before the Law (Gen 14:20) and confirmed after the Law (Matthew 23:23). However, a better approach is what many Christians today practice: Grace giving instead of Tithing.

People with well-intentioned involvement in multiple ministries often wonder if it is okay to split their tithe between their church and another ministry. No one can stop you, but *Nehemiah 10:37 says that the Levites are to gather the tithe locally.* That requires us to give where we eat. You should have a home church that you are active in. There is nothing wrong, however, with sending offerings to TV, radio, or outreach ministries. Many of the leaders' people send money to, will tell you to give to your home church first, then help others. Others want to divert their giving to God to support elderly parents or the poor. 2 Corinthians 12:14 mentions that Children are not responsible for saving up for their parents, but parents are responsible for their children. However, there are times when, due to poor stewardship or life's circumstances, children must step in to support their parents. As stewards, we know that the tithe does not belong to us, but it belongs to the Lord. Part of giving is learning to trust the Lord. However, please consult with your priest or pastor and seek their counsel. Most will likely tell you to care for your parents. Deferring what God requires is a matter of prayer, and sometimes it is a matter of your heart. We never want to miss out on what God has in store for us.

Some churches give to larger churches. Hebrews 7:7, when speaking about authority, says, *"The lesser is blessed by the greater."* Therefore, churches under leadership may give something upward. *Numbers 18:26* reads *"speak to the Levites and say to them, 'When you take from the sons of Israel the tithe which I have given you from them for your inheritance, then you shall present an offering from it to the LORD, a tithe of the tithe.* Even those who receive financial gifts from others must also give in return.

A BETTER WAY

. . . . .

Grace giving is a term that means Spirit-led giving. Grace-giving means you open your treasury (2 Kings 20:15) and let God take out what he wants. The new covenant believer is to be led by the Holy Spirit in all things, including giving. When the Spirit-led receive their income, they ask God what He wants them to give, and then they give that amount. I should warn you, though God is in the habit of stretching your faith to the limits. The average church that practices tithing receives less than 4% of the members' income. Grace-giving churches typically receive 5% more of their members' income than do churches that require tithing. In short, Spirit-led giving surpasses law-based giving. They are using the New Testament model of being led by God in everything. So be careful what you wish for when discussing the New Testament giving. If you become a grace-giver, expect the Lord to challenge you to give more than ever before.

Scan to watch video: A Lifestyle to Bless

CHAPTER SEVEN

THE TREASURE PRINCIPLE

. . . .

TITUS 2:14

Who gave himself for us, that he might redeem us from all iniquity and purify for himself a people for his own possession, zealous for good works.

THE DIFFERENCE BETWEEN TITHES AND OFFERINGS

The primary difference between tithes and offerings is that Israel used tithes for ministry, not **SACRIFICE (Surrendering A Consecrated Redemptive Item Faithfully Invokes Christ Example)**. Tithes are required giving and are used to provide for the affairs of Israel. The Levites stored the tithe, whether it was from the herd or grain, for future use. Tithing is not part of the sacrificial system; offerings are. The sacrificial system was about giving something away to gain something of greater value in return. The Israelites gave tithes from their herds and grain to sustain the ongoing ministry. Priest received offerings from those same herds and grain after collecting the tithe. One was mandatory, and the other was optional and redemptive. Like tithes, offerings are given only to the Lord. Exodus 22:20 reads, *"He who sacrifices to any god, except to Yahweh only, shall be utterly destroyed."* Offerings are sacrifices made to God. They are not required but redemptive. The Israelites freely offered gifts, and each had a different redemptive purpose. Neither the tithe nor offerings were in money except when we exceeded the value of the tithe to give it a redemptive quality, as we previously discussed in Leviticus 27:31. Therefore, everything above the 10% tithe is a redemptive offering.

Many people give less than 10% of their income, still reasoning in their hearts and minds that they are giving both tithes and offerings. Sadly, they are mistaken. Sacrifice begins where requirement ends. Anything you give freely that goes beyond what is required is a sacrifice. We go above and beyond when we give anything over one-tenth of our income. For one reason or another, most believers either never reach or do not stay at that level. While tithing is a duty based upon our relationship with God. Offering is a voluntary act based upon the love we have for our God.

Remember, I said that redemption deals with reconnecting, restoring, resanctifying, reconciling, restituting, repairing, and recommitting. The word Redemption means "to loosen or deliver from bondage by paying the price". The price is the amount of substance required to purchase or ransom back what's in bondage. What I mean by 'Redemptive Giving' is that it signifies the purpose of an offering. As we said, offerings are going beyond the expected giving. Just as the tithe has its purpose for maintaining the covenant, so do these offerings have their purpose. In Job 1:5, Job regularly gave offerings for his children in case one might sin and curse God in their heart, which was the very thing Satan later tried to get Job to do. Job made offerings to God to ensure his children did not offend God with their actions. If you study the offerings in the bible, there has always been a redemptive nature to them. That is to say that each offering served a particular purpose in freeing the one giving the offering from some spiritual, social, or physical bondage.

OLD TESTAMENT OFFERINGS

Leviticus 17:11 For the life of the flesh is in the blood. I have given it to you on the altar to make atonement for your souls; for it is the blood that makes atonement by reason of the life.

The sacrificial system of Israel allowed redemption to occur through the offering of clean animals and sacrificial substances that represented life as a substitute for the one who had offended. Many believe sacrifice is about offering the death of the animal, when it is about the life of the animal. Sacrifices offer life, as the scriptures say, life is in the blood. Sacrifice was the law's autocorrective system, designed to delay judgment for the people's offenses, offering **to REDEEM (Restoration Extended Defeats Every Effort Made)** them. There were ten Old Testament sacrifices, consisting of five bloodied sacrifices and five unbloody sacrifices, that represented a greater sacrifice. Each sacrifice fulfilled a different purpose and function. An additional two offerings based on the actions the priest was to apply, bring the total number of offerings to twelve. The priest offered the sacrifices in various ways and for several reasons, all of which were redemptive in nature. As a pastor, I find that most believers and leaders lack a clear understanding of the actual sacrifices and their significance. A thorough explanation would require its own book, and if the Lord allows, I will someday write one about the sacrificial system. However, just reading this chapter will probably cause you to know more about the sacrificial system than 90% of believers.

THE FIVE BLOODIED SACRIFICES
Burnt Offerings - Repairing Relationship

> *Leviticus 1:4 He shall lay his hand on the head of the burnt offering, and it shall be accepted for him to make atonement for him.*

The burnt offering comes from a word that means an offering that ascends to heaven through burning, atoning for a broken relationship. The priest sacrificed a clean animal on the altar, offering it as a burnt offering for the people. The purpose of the burnt offering is to bring atonement. Atonement means precisely what it says: at-one-ment. It is a redemptive price paid to fix the problem in our relationship with God. Atonement is the act of covering and restoring the harmony between God and humanity after wrongdoing or injury. Jesus made the ultimate atonement sacrifice for us on the cross.

The Peace Offering – Reconciling Offenders

> *Leviticus 3:7 If he offers a lamb for his offering, then he shall offer it before Yahweh; and he shall lay his hand on the head of his offering, and kill it before the Tent of Meeting. Aaron's sons shall sprinkle its blood around on the altar.*

Contrary to popular belief, not all offerings were males of the flock. The peace offering, also known as the fellowship offering, could be either male or female (Leviticus 3:1) and was intended to restore fellowship with God, often being offered as a thanksgiving offering. The Levitical priests would offer a fellowship offering in conjunction with a burnt, sin, or freewill offering, accompanied by unleavened bread (Leviticus 7:12). The priest dedicated a portion of this offering to God, with another portion reserved for the priest to eat. In the peace offering, the donor would receive back a portion of what they gave, since it was, they who were asking for peace. The redemptive purpose was to bring about reconciliation between the two parties in conflict. Thereby establishing peace and fellowship.

The Sin Offering – Restoring The Soul

Leviticus 4:2=3 Speak to the children of Israel, saying, 'If anyone sins unintentionally, in any of the things which Yahweh has commanded not to be done, and does any one of them, if the anointed priest sins so as to bring guilt on the people, then let him offer for his sin which he has sinned a young bull without defect to Yahweh for a sin offering.

A sin offering is an offering made for an unintentional sin. Yes, you heard that right, unintentional sin. These are unintentional sins people committed because they lacked knowledge that what they were doing was sinful. Intentional sins like rebellion, or those with forethought, are dealt with only through repentance, even in the Old Testament. These were sins against God's authority. Since many people have not thoroughly studied the sacrificial system, you often hear people say, 'If you sin, you offer a sacrifice. The truth is that if you sin, you confess and repent. Only after cleaning the soul could, you offer a sacrifice. The sin offering restores the soul to a proper position with God. Leviticus 4:28 states, "*If his sin which he has sinned is made known to him, then he shall bring for his offering a goat, a female without defect, for his sin which he has sinned.*" If a priest, ruler, or the entire congregation of Israel sinned, they would have to bring a male sin offering. That is why Jesus takes away the sins of the world. However, if ordinary or everyday people sinned individually, a female offering was sacrificed.

The Guilt Offering – Restitution for Offense

> *Leviticus 5:15 If anyone commits a trespass, and sins unwittingly regarding Yahweh's holy things, then he shall bring his trespass offering to Yahweh: a ram without defect from the flock, according to your estimation in silver by shekels, according to the shekel of the sanctuary, for a trespass offering.*

The Guilt offering, also called the trespass offering, is related to the Sin offering with one exception. Both are unintentional sins, but the guilt offering deals with violations of things set apart for God's purposes. The very next verse states that the one committing the guilt offering must make restitution for the wrong done to the holy things (Leviticus 5:16). Unlike the sin offering, which was a sin against God's authority, these were sins against God's holiness. Defiling what was holy was a serious offense. Those who did so deliberately would often die, as was the case when the men of Beth Shemesh looked inside the ark of the covenant (1 Samuel 6:19). In cases of accidental defilement, God allowed the trespass offering as an attempt to make them safe by requiring restitution.

The Red Heifer – Sanctifying the Holy

> *Numbers 19:8-9 He who burns her shall wash his clothes in water, and bathe his flesh in water, and shall be unclean until the even. A clean man shall gather up the ashes of the heifer, and lay them up outside of the camp in a clean place; and it shall be kept for the congregation of the children of Israel for use in water for cleansing impurity. It is a sin offering.*

The final bloodied offering is the red heifer. The red heifer offering is a sin offering that isn't for offenses but for cleansing and sanctifying. The sin, peace, and guilt offerings could be either male or female (Leviticus 3:1, 4:28 & 5:5); however, the red heifer offering was the only mandatory female offering, just as the burnt offering is the only mandatory male-only offering. This lack of understanding is why I shudder when I hear people preach that the offerings had to be a male from the flock. Four of the five bloodied offerings could be female animals from the flock. The one who killed the red heifer became unclean, but when another priest gathered the ashes, those ashes sanctified everything they touched.

THE 5 UNBLOODIED OFFERINGS

The Grain Offering - Reconnect

> *Leviticus 2:11 No grain offering that you present to the LORD may be made with leaven, for you are not to burn any leaven or honey as an offering made by fire to the LORD.*

Grain Offerings, also called the meal offering, are always given in conjunction with other offerings. It is the first of the two unbloodied sacrificial substances. The meal offering is an offering of unleavened bread, in which the priest offers the memorial portion to God and eats the rest (Leviticus 2:9). The unleavened bread reconnects the people with God, as they share a meal with Him. God brought His presence closer to those who partook of this fellowship or communion meal. The memorial portions of this unleavened bread offering mentioned in verses 2, 9 & 16 are essential because this is what Jesus spoke of when He said in Luke 22:19, *"This is my body, do this in remembrance of me."*

The Drink Offering - Recommit

> *Numbers 15:5 With the burnt offering or sacrifice of each lamb, you are to prepare a quarter hin of wine as a drink offering.*

The second offering of a sacrificial substance in place of a bloodied sacrifice is the drink offering. It is an offering of wine. Like the meal offering, the drink or libation offering accompanies another type of offering. Philippians 2:17 mentions this when Paul spoke about his expectant death in service to Christ, saying, *"But even if I am being poured out like a drink offering on the sacrifice and service of your faith, I am glad and rejoice with all of you."* The drink offering represented the total commitment of your life, and the Israelites used this offering when making covenants. Christ used the third cup of the Passover meal, known as the cup of redemption, as a drink offering of His blood, thereby establishing a new covenant in His blood (Mark 14:24). The Drink and Grain offering is part of an offering formula representative of Christ's body and blood or a prefigurement of His sacrifice and of communion.

I should mention that while the bloody sacrifices are redemptive, the unbloody sacrifices deal with rituals that represent something greater.

Jesus connected the grain and libation offerings — bread and wine — to the future eucharistic meal we call communion, thereby closely associating them with the bloody sacrifice on the cross. The remaining offerings are not to be connected with the blood sacrifice on the cross but with an offering of our service to God.

The Incense Offering - Relationship

Malachi 1:11 For from the rising of the sun even to its going down, my name is great among the nations, and in every place incense will be offered to my name, and a pure offering; for my name is great among the nations," says Yahweh of Armies.

The Incense Offering would be offered on the altar of Incense in the temple and represented the prayers of the people. At the time of this offering, the people would be gathered in the temple courts, locked in prayer for themselves and their nation. We see this practice mentioned when Zacharias was in the temple, burning incense on the altar of incense, as stated in Luke 1:10: *"The whole multitude of the people were praying outside at the hour of incense."* Incense was also offered locally in censers by priests and accompanied the prayers of the people.

The Ordination Offering - Consecration

Leviticus 8:28 Moses took them from their hands, and burned them on the altar on the burnt offering. They were a consecration offering for a pleasant aroma. It was an offering made by fire to Yahweh.

The passage above refers to Moses ordaining and anointing the sons of Aaron as priests. Using the burnt offering, which represented total commitment, the ordination offering, also known as the consecration offering, is a burnt offering presented to set people apart exclusively to do the work of God. It was an offering on behalf of those who would dedicate themselves exclusively to serving God's work. Jesus Himself served as the ordaining offering for the apostles by giving Himself up and breathing upon them, saying, "Receive the Holy Spirit," and giving them the authority to declare His forgiveness (John 20:22-23).

The Offering of Salt - Obedience

> *Leviticus 2:13 Every offering of your meal offering you shall season with salt. You shall not allow the salt of the covenant of your God to be lacking from your meal offering. With all your offerings you shall offer salt.*

The priest offered salt, representing the covenant, with every meal or meat offering. Salt was a binding obligation that permeated every offering, impacting everything the Lord received. From Numbers 18:19, we understand that the covenant of salt represents something that is forever before Yahweh. We are to include it because it is something that can never be lost. We can say much about salt, keeping the offering pure and preserved; however, the key is obedience. God didn't need to give a reason for the covenant of salt. He said to do it, and just like that —bam —they did it.

THE ADDITIONAL TWO - DEDICATION OFFERINGS

Two offerings listed in the Bible are signified not by what you give, but by the manner in which the priest presents them. These are the Wave and Heave offerings. Have you ever visited a church where the priest stands with the offering of Christ's body and blood, hands lifted or waving the offering while reciting a prayer or a vow? These acts consecrate and dedicate the offering to the Lord.

The Wave Offering - Communing

> *Numbers 18:11 This is yours, too: the wave offering of their gift, even all the wave offerings of the children of Israel. I have given them to you, and to your sons and to your daughters with you, as a portion forever. Everyone who is clean in your house shall eat of it.*

The wave offering was an offering lifted and waved before the Lord as an act of worship. Wave offerings were offerings that the priest participated in and could eat from. It was waved toward the altar, signifying that it was offered to the Lord, then back from the altar, indicating that the priest was receiving it back as a gift from God. The right to participate makes Holy **COMMUNION (Covenant Ordained Memorial Meal Uniting Neighbors In Our Nation)** not just an offering you lift, but one gently waved as a presentation before the Lord. We will discuss First Fruits in the next chapter, but it was a wave offering where the priest waved the sheaf of grain early in the morning on the first day of the week (Sunday) after the Passover. Passover Sunday is the day Jesus resurrected and revealed Himself as a wave offering.

The Heave Offering – Receiving

> *Numbers 5:9 Every heave offering of all the holy things of the children of Israel, which they present to the priest, shall be his.*

The heave offering is an offering of return. The heave offering is lifted to the Lord and then lowered to give it back for the use of the kingdom. It consisted of any sacred thing that God wanted to be used and not destroyed on the altar. The freewill offering given to Moses to build the tabernacle was a heave offering. The heave offering could be animal sacrifices given to the priest or money for the temple. Numbers 18:24 says that the tithe is a heave offering. Heave offerings were presented to God at the altar, sanctifying them for use in His kingdom. Many churches give thanks and pray over the giving of the people as a heave offering based on 1 Timothy 4:4-5, stating, *"For every creature of God is good, and nothing is to be rejected if it is received with thanksgiving. For it is sanctified through the word of God and prayer."*

REDEMPTION FROM SPIRITUAL BONDAGE

> *Hebrews 10:8-10 Previously saying, "Sacrifices and offerings and whole burnt offerings and sacrifices for sin you didn't desire, neither had pleasure in them" (those which are offered according to the law), then he has said, "Behold, I have come to do your will." He takes away the first, that he may establish the second, by which will we have been sanctified through the offering of the body of Jesus Christ once for all.*

Jesus came to establish the will of God, which is obedience. Speaking to King Saul, 1 Samuel 15:22 says, Samuel said, *"Has Yahweh as great delight in burnt offerings and sacrifices, as in obeying Yahweh's voice? Behold, to obey is better than sacrifice, and to listen than the fat of rams."* The sacrificial system served a corrective function, relieving punishment and restoring the worshipper to a state of grace. God prefers that we obey, and there would be no need to offer sacrifice. It is our spiritual bondage to sin that is the problem. The beginning of our release from this bondage began with a greater sacrifice.

Isaiah 53 gives us the clearest picture of Jesus Christ's work in redeeming us. As stewards of God, we give offerings willingly. Isaiah not only pictures Jesus as the Suffering Servant (or Steward) but also as the sacrificial lamb who willingly gave His life. Jesus was the Sacrifice that God gave, laid on a wooden altar called the **CROSS (Christ Redemptively Offers Spiritual Sacrifice)**. The cross was God's ultimate act of love toward humanity. With it, we can join in with the words of John the Baptist in John 1:29, when he declared, "Behold the Lamb of God who takes away the sin of the world." The bible tells us that Christ gave Himself up for us so that He may redeem us. Jesus redeemed His church by paying the ransom price, freeing us from the bondage and penalty of our sins. Jesus was offered up to God the Father on our behalf as a substitute and atonement for our sin.

When I look at nativity scenes, I think of the offering God made for our redemption. The Old Testament offering system foreshadowed the redemption Christ brought us on the cross. He is our New Testament **OFFERING (One Forgiven Finds Eternal Redemption In Nativity's Gift)**. Romans 8:3-4 reads *"For what the law couldn't do, in that it was weak through the flesh, God did, sending his own Son in the likeness of sinful flesh and for sin, he condemned sin in the flesh, that the ordinance of the law might be fulfilled in us who don't walk according to the flesh, but according to the Spirit."*. The Law of God isn't weak; it is perfect in converting the soul, as recorded in Psalm 19:7. Still, the issue with the law is that our flesh desires loopholes. Romans 7:8 says, *"But sin, finding occasion through the commandment, produced in me all kinds of coveting. For apart from the law, sin is dead."* The very fact that a law existed stirred humanity's immaturity. The rebellious nature of sin exploits the law, intensifying our sinful desires. However, Jesus was God's solution, as Colossians 1:20 states, *"and through him to reconcile all things to himself by him, whether things on the earth or things in the heavens, having made peace through the blood of his cross."*

FINANCIAL CONFESSION

· · · · ·

Sacrifice and confession were inseparable. Whenever the Israelites made a sacrificial offering, they confessed the reason for it and what they wanted to occur. Since sacrifices are redemptive, our confession guides the redemptive purpose we receive.

Heavenly Father, forgive me for participation in any wasteful or debt-causing habits that have affected my financial position. I ask for your wisdom and guidance in managing my finances and doing what is pleasing to you. Help me understand your will and enhance my financial literacy so I can make informed choices as your steward. Break any strongholds of financial insecurity that attempt to enter into my family line. Grant us the plan to establish and maintain generational wealth, and a heart that enables us to give as we receive.

Grant my family the understanding of the sons of Issachar who understood the times and seasons in Israel. Cause us to grow in wisdom and stature as well as favor with God and man. Establish my home on a firm foundation where we can live a faithful but quiet life, work with our hands, and keep to the business that you have given us. I pray the leading of your Holy Spirit in all our endeavors and that we please you, remaining in your love, in the name of Jesus Christ. Amen.

Scan to watch video: Living Sacrifices

CHAPTER EIGHT

THE GENEROSITY HABIT

· · · · · · · · · · · ·

WAIT A MINUTE

Didn't we forget to mention the Freewill Offering? No, we didn't. We just made a strategic move to generosity. Beyond the redemptive and ritualistic reasons for offerings lies the **GENEROUS (Gifts Economic Needs Earnestly Reviewed Offers Unselfish Sacrifice)** heart. It is an offering of rejoicing because we love God. Like the widow giving her two mites, the freewill offering always receives the recognition of God. Generosity happens even when there is no personal reason to be generous There were only 12 tribes in Israel still, when Jacob saw the two sons of Joseph he crossed his hands praying for them, adopting them as sons eventually stating, *"Moreover I have given to you one portion above your brothers, which I took out of the hand of the Amorite with my sword and with my bow* (Genesis 48:22)." This adoption created 13 tribes where there were 12. The same concept occurs with the Freewill Offerings. It came later, after God gave instructions on building the tabernacle. It is the extra child of offerings where you give just because you want to.

Christ fulfilled all seven redemptive offerings; thus, the church no longer practices them today. The ritual offerings are still used in some form, even if the prescribed incense formula, originally intended only for the Levitical priests, is no longer used in current censers, and the ashes used in some ordinations have a different source. However, churches still practice free-will offerings as a heartfelt gesture of love today. A dedicated steward offers the freewill offering. Informing the church in Corinth about the Macedonian churches' commitment, 2 Corinthians 8:3-5 says, *"For according to their power, I testify, yes and beyond their power, they gave of their own accord, begging us with much entreaty to receive this grace and the fellowship in the service to the saints. This was not as we had expected, but first they gave their own selves to the Lord, and to us through the will of God."* Giving of resources isn't hard when you first give yourself to God. The church gave itself to God first, then followed its leadership, before giving to those in need. They serve as a great testimony to Christian freewill giving.

Not only is the freewill offering from a good heart, but it also comes from a heart stirred by God. Ezra 1:5-6 reads, *"Then the heads of fathers' households of Judah and Benjamin, the priests and the Levites, all whose spirit God had stirred to go up, rose up to build Yahweh's house which is in Jerusalem. All those who were around them strengthened their hands with vessels of silver, with gold, with goods, with animals, and with precious things, in addition to all that was willingly offered."* After the Babylonian captivity ended, some were stirred to return to Jerusalem to work and to give freewill offerings. According to Exodus 35:29, freewill offerings are for doing the work of the Lord. All of God's work is a work of the heart. Love motivates and inspires us. As faithful stewards, we set our hearts on God and His kingdom, working, giving, and doing what we can to see His kingdom come.

THE BIG DIFFERENCE IN FREEWILL OFFERINGS.

In the Old Testament, there were famines and deaths for offering something defective to God. One significant difference between freewill offerings and other offerings is that freewill offerings do not have to be perfect. Yes, some offerings can have flaws. Leviticus 22:23-24 states, *"You may present as a freewill offering an ox or sheep that has a deformed or stunted limb, but it is not acceptable in fulfillment of a vow. You are not to present to the LORD an animal whose testicles are bruised, crushed, torn, or cut; you are not to sacrifice them in your land."* God accepted deformed animals and ones with stunted growth as freewill offerings, but only those that could still reproduce. Remember, reproduction is what makes our finances work, just like a seed. While I believe we should always give God our best. At our best, all of our righteousness is as filthy rags. With freewill, offering God accepts what you have without reproach. 2 Corinthians 8:12 states, *"For if the readiness is there, it is acceptable according to what you have, not according to what you don't have."* We should all give, but we shouldn't make people feel bad about not being able to give more than they can afford.

A GENEROUS GIFT OF FIRST FRUITS

> *Exodus 34:22 You shall observe the feast of weeks with the first fruits of wheat harvest, and the feast of harvest at the year's end.*

The Feast of Weeks was a time of celebration and of sacrifice. One of the main components of the feast was the giving of First Fruits. You may be beginning to ask, 'What are First Fruits?' First Fruits is an offering given to God at the time of the harvest. The people of Israel would take the first-ripened fruit of the harvest and offer it to God in thanks for his provision throughout the previous year. This offering showed God gratitude for what He had done, with an expectancy of what He would do in the following year. As stewards of God, the first of everything we have belongs to Him. Nehemiah 10:37 states, *"and that we should bring the first fruits of our dough, our wave offerings, the fruit of all kinds of trees, and the new wine and the oil, to the priests, to the rooms of the house of our God; and the tithes of our ground to the Levites; for they, the Levites, take the tithes in all our farming villages."* First Fruits is more than giving the first of the harvest. It is a way to **BLESS (Believers Listening Earn Spiritual Substance)** God. It is giving the first of the prepared dough that you make, from the wave offering that you receive back, and the first of the batch of wine and oil after they are refined.

Exodus 13:1-2 *goes* even further, saying, *"Yahweh spoke to Moses, saying, Sanctify to me all the firstborn, whatever opens the womb among the children of Israel, both of man and of animal. It is mine."* The Israelites dedicated the first of everything to God. Later, instead of taking the firstborn of Israel, He told them He would call the tribe of Levi to serve Him. Numbers 3:12 *Behold, I have taken the Levites from among the children of Israel instead of all the firstborn who open the womb among the children of Israel; and the Levites shall be mine."* Whether it is the firstborn child, the firstborn animal, raw fruit, grains, or processed food, the first of everything belongs to the Lord. The First Fruits was the Old Testament way of seeking first the kingdom of God and His righteousness so that He would add to them all that they required.

HOW TO GIVE FIRST FRUITS

First Fruits are giving God, the **FIRST (Foremost Initiating Receives Spiritual Triumph)** of everything we receive from Him. It is an acknowledgement that everything we have is a gift from God. As I have said, the first of everything belongs to God, and He requires His Stewards to bring it in annually. Nehemiah 10:35 reads *"and to bring the first fruits of our ground and the first fruits of all fruit of all kinds of trees, year by year, to*

Yahweh's house." This yearly time brought much provision into the house of God. First Fruits would cause abundance to flow in God's house, allowing not only for the priest to be cared for, but also for the poor and widows.

Deuteronomy 26:2 reads *" that you shall take some of the first of all the fruit of the ground, which you shall bring in from your land that Yahweh your God gives you. You shall put it in a basket, and shall go to the place which Yahweh your God shall choose to cause his name to dwell there".* The people brought their First Fruits to the place that God set apart to establish His name. Today, this would be representative of a healthy, well-balanced local church congregation. Leviticus 23:11 informs us that after the priest receives the first fruits, *"He shall wave the sheaf before Yahweh, to be accepted for you. On the next day after the Sabbath the priest shall wave it."* The priest presents First Fruits as a wave offering to God on the day after the Sabbath, which is on a Sunday. Note that the Jewish Sabbath is observed from Friday evening to Saturday evening, not Sunday, which is the Lord's day, in most Christian Churches. The Early Christian church met daily. They later began meeting on Sunday as a celebration of the Lord's resurrection from the Dead.

THE SIGN OF GOD'S REDEMPTION

Exodus 13:15-16 When Pharaoh stubbornly refused to let us go, Yahweh killed all the firstborn in the land of Egypt, both the firstborn of man, and the firstborn of livestock. Therefore I sacrifice to Yahweh all that opens the womb, being males; but all the firstborn of my sons I redeem.' It shall be for a sign on your hand, and for symbols between your eyes; for by strength of hand Yahweh brought us out of Egypt.

As we discussed in our last chapter on redemptive giving, God is a deliverer. Jesus redeemed us through his vicarious death. The sign of that redemption is that we put God first in all things. The Bible says that giving God the firstborn is like a sign on your hand and a symbol on your forehead. Exodus 13:9 says, *"It shall be for a sign to you on your hand, and for a memorial between your eyes, that Yahweh's law may be in your mouth; for with a strong hand Yahweh has brought you out of Egypt."* First fruits are not a mark, but rather a symbol that everything we have belongs to God. First Fruits are a reminder to the believer that God is sovereign and that His word is on our lips and in our hearts. Out of the abundance of the heart the mouth does speak (Matthew 12:34).

These signs are reminiscent of the signs listed in Revelation 13:16-17 which says, *"He causes all, the small and the great, the rich and the poor, and the free and the slave, to be given marks on their right hands or on their foreheads; and that no one would be able to buy or to sell unless he has that mark, which is the name of the beast or the number of his name."* The sign God placed to represent the deliverance of Israel will become the place that Satan places his mark. Satan, being an imitator, will one day mark people in the same manner. Those who accept the mark of the beast will, in fact, be saying, "You Satan are my deliverer and I will put you before all else". This replacement worship is the kind the Beast will receive from men during the tribulation period.

When the children of Israel entered the land, they were to give a first-fruits offering on the first day of the week after the Passover. Leviticus 23:15-16 *"You shall count from the next day after the Sabbath, from the day that you brought the sheaf of the wave offering: seven Sabbaths shall be completed. The next day after the seventh Sabbath you shall count fifty days; and you shall offer a new meal offering to Yahweh".* The Jews celebrated Pentecost, also known as the Feast of Weeks, fifty days after the Passover Sunday. The word Pentecost means fifty. This is significant because the Bible says in Mark 16:9-11, " *Now when he had risen early on the first day of the week, he appeared first to Mary Magdalene, from whom he had cast out seven demons. She went and told those who had been with him, as they mourned and wept. When they heard that he was alive and had been seen by her, they disbelieved.*" This is how we know that Jesus Christ rose from the dead at the celebration of First Fruits and presented Himself victoriously.

GOD'S FIRST FRUITS GIFTS

Have you thought that all this giving is just too much? The great thing about our God is that you can never beat Him in giving. Everything we give to God, He gives back to us even more. God has also given First Fruits to believers. The most crucial first fruit is Jesus' sacrificial death. 1 Corinthians 15:20-21 says, "*But now Christ has been raised from the dead. He became the first fruit of those who are asleep. For since death came by man, the resurrection of the dead also came by man.*" As we just mentioned, Jesus' resurrection is God's First Fruits offering. Because Christ rose from the dead as the first ripe fruit on the vine, we will rise as the latter fruit. James 1:18 speaks about our position with God, stating, "*Of his own will he gave birth to us by the word of truth, that we should be a kind of first fruits of his creatures.*". James tells us that believers are the first fruits of God's creatures. First Fruits represent the special relationship between God and the church. God desires to be first in our lives, and He puts us first or preeminent in His eternal life.

Another aspect of God calling His people as a firstfruit is evident in our ministry and evangelistic efforts. 1 Corinthians 16:15 says, "*Now I beg you, brothers—you know the house of Stephanas, that it is the first fruits of Achaia, and that they have set themselves to serve the saints.*" Stephanas' household was not only the first to accept the gospel in Achaia, but they also worked hard to dedicate themselves to the work of ministry. As servants, we ease the burden of the work on the rest of the saints. However, people are not the only gift God gives; He also gives Himself to His people. Romans 8:23 says, "*Not only so, but ourselves also, who have the first fruits of the Spirit, even we ourselves groan within ourselves, waiting for adoption, the redemption of our body.*" God gave us the power, anointing, and sanctifying work of the Holy Spirit in our lives as a firstfruits and foreshadowing of what we will be like in our glorified bodies. We have only caught a glimpse of what the Lord has in store for us. He is generous, so that we can be generous to others.

THE BLESSING OF FIRST FRUITS

As in everything involved in stewardship, it comes down to wisdom and faithfulness. Are you faithful in giving God the first and the best? Are you wise enough to take advantage of the blessings that come from First Fruits? First Fruits comes with several blessings or reasons to give. The first is that it leaves a blessing on your finances. Numbers 15:21 states, " *Of the first of your dough, you shall give to Yahweh a wave offering throughout your generations.*" This wave offering is the First Fruits, where the Jewish nation was to give the first portion to God. We gain understanding when we connect the first of your dough wave offering to the New Testament in Romans 11:16, which states, "*If the first fruit is holy, so is the lump. If the root is holy, so are the branches.*" Giving the first portion of your finances to God will make all your future finances for that year holy. First Fruits causes God to treat your finances as holy, giving you favor with God because He connects your finances for the rest of the year to the First Fruits offering.

A second reason is that it causes a blessing to rest on your household. Ezekiel 44:30 states, " *The first of all the first fruits of every thing, and every offering of everything, of all your offerings, shall be for the priest. You shall also give to the priests the first of your dough, to cause a blessing to rest on your house.*" Not only will God bless your **FINANCES (Funding Involves New Assets Netting Currency Effectively Shared)**, but also your home. The word blessed means happy. Often, a financial blessing is not our primary need or concern. Having a blessing on your home positions you to experience healing in your physical, spiritual, and emotional needs, for you and your family. When you give First Fruits, not only do you benefit, but your saved and unsaved loved ones do as well.

The last and most important reason to give First Fruits is that it is an act of worship. Proverbs 3:9-10 says, *"Honor Jehovah with thy substance, And with the first-fruits of all thine increase: So shall thy barns be filled with plenty, And thy vats shall overflow with new wine"*. First Fruits bring honor to God. By giving the first to God, we are showing Him that He is the most important one in our lives. It also activates the principle of living a life more in abundance. As mentioned in chapter one, 20 percent of the world's billionaires are Jewish, even when they are 0,2% of the world's population. They still practice First Fruits because the offering doesn't require the temple. In recent years, several individuals and churches have also started this practice. At the turn of the year or the start of a new job or business venture, they give a portion of the first earnings to God, so the Lord will bless everything that comes. It doesn't mean the person stops being a regular giver; it means they make themselves a priority giver before God. Yes, some do so for the money, while others do it for the blessing.

THOUGHTS ABOUT FIRST FRUITS

The first question people ask about First Fruits is, "why are they hardly mentioned in Christian circles?" Don't be shocked; many things, such as the 20-20-30 tithe, aren't mentioned in churches. It is right there in the Bible, and I believe that God doesn't give you information to know it, but to do it. Now that you know what you do is what matters. While many churches practice giving first fruits, there have also been abuses of this practice. Some ministries have turned First Fruits into a fundraiser. While First Fruits provides for ministry, its primary purpose is to teach believers always to put God first, just as He put us first by sending Christ. Scriptures list three uses for First Fruits in the kingdom of God. First, they provide for the priest according to Numbers 18:12. Secondly, Deuteronomy 26:11 lists it as a benevolence fund to care for widows and orphans. Lastly, it can be used as an emergency fund or storehouse for times of need or disaster relief, as mentioned in Nehemiah 10:33 & 39.

If the church observes First Fruits Sunday, at the very least, they should receive the gift in a basket, pray for the giver, and pronounce a blessing, such as the Aaronic blessing in Numbers 6:22-27 or another biblical blessing. The people gave First Fruits at the time of the Harvest. Since Passover began on the 14th of Nisan on the Jewish calendar, the Feast of First Fruits always falls on the third Sunday of the Jewish New Year. Sometimes, when people change jobs, receive an inheritance, or sell property, they want to give a First Fruits offering on it. It is a personal decision, as First Fruits were the only required offering; however, they based the amount on free-will. The Jewish Talmud (Terumoth 4:3) specifies a minimum amount of one-sixtieth part as the first-fruits offering. However, that was one of three harvests of the year. Making it as low as two days' pay, while some I know give as high as a week's earnings. The most important thing is that it reflects generosity because giving to God always works when done from a heart of love. The steward is not the owner. Giving God what is His first is not a question of reciprocity but the answer of faithfulness.

We have spent a significant amount of time explaining what the Bible actually teaches about tithing, offerings, and what New Testament giving means: being led by the Holy Spirit. Stewardship is about properly handling resources. That requires us to maximize our earnings, take care of what we have, avoid overspending, and adhere to a financial **PLAN (Proposed Lesson: Achieving Needs)**. Proper stewardship prepares and positions us for promotion. Let's get ready to spend less and live more.

MAKE A SIMPLE FINANCIAL PLAN IN 7 STEPS

· · · · ·

A financial plan is an outline of your financial standing and goals used to measure progress.

1. Determine your net worth and gather 3 months of bank statements to review your spending and identify areas where you can save money.
2. Use DART to set your financial goals and create a budget that you can stick to. Remember, what you do today is financing your future.
3. Save an emergency fund at a bank a few miles away where you don't have a debit card. Making it more difficult to withdraw gives you time to think before you spend.
4. Stop creating new debt, make a plan to pay off current debt, and don't give up.
5. Organize investments and retirement preparations. Estimate what you will need for the future, then add 10% to that.
6. Place property in a trust and get insurance for your assets (home, vehicle, health, life, disability)
7. Review routinely. Readjust your tactics. Remind yourself of your goals.

Scan to watch video: You're Second

CHAPTER NINE

SPENDING LESS AND LIVING MORE

. . . .

PROVERBS 21:20

I There is precious treasure and oil in the dwelling
of the wise, but a foolish man swallows it up.

HOW MONEY WORKS

Money is a medium of exchange that stores value based on societal acceptance and recognition. Money replaced the barter system, in which people exchanged goods directly for other goods —for example, if I exchanged a bag of beans for a pair of pants supplied by another person. The barter system, when applied subjectively, assigned value based on personal need and required that goods be on hand to make the exchange. Money replaced the barter system as a means for the government to set values, rather than individuals. Government-issued currency, referred to as "fiat" money, derives its value from the government instead of from the fundamental demand for the commodity. The dollar retains value because the government designates it as legal tender. Since money relies on consensus, physical currency can be any tangible object or exist solely in electronic form. Digital cryptocurrencies, such as Bitcoin, can be considered a form of money if individuals accept them in exchange for goods and services.

PREPARATION FOR A PROBLEM

One of the hardest, yet equally important, things for a steward to do is save. Everyone can save, whether it is spare change, $20, or $200 a month. Many people live paycheck to paycheck, and if their income is disrupted, such as by losing their job, it can be a disaster. Savings give you a cushion to breathe in case of a tragedy or if your car breaks down. The story of Pharaoh and Joseph in Genesis 41 is one of the greatest examples of why we should save. We all have famines in our lives. Famines are times of economic troubles. Do you know the solution God gave to Pharaoh through Joseph??? **SAVINGS (Securing Assets Valued Increases Nest-egg Growth Strategy)**. Usually, when we get a little extra money, we spend it. God is saying no, put it away. The extra money saved during our prosperous times is usually enough to sustain us through our times of famine. If we prepare for eventualities, then we may not suffer as much when they come. Everyone knows they should save, but too few do. Proverbs 6:6-8 says, *"Go to the ant, you sluggard. Consider her ways, and be wise; which having no chief, overseer, or ruler, provides her bread in the summer, and gathers her food in the harvest."* In plentiful times, the Steward should put away all they can, and in lean times, put away what they can.

The 80/20 rule mentioned in chapter 4 is related to the plan God gave Joseph to save Egypt and the surrounding regions from a coming disaster. God gave Joseph the interpretation of Pharaoh's dreams, which indicated that seven sickly cows and blighted heads of grain would consume the seven fat cows and seven healthy heads of grain that came before them. The dream meant that Egypt would experience seven years of prosperity, followed by a seven-year famine so severe that people would forget the prosperity they once enjoyed. Joseph's solution was the 80/20 rule: live off 80% of what you earn, and the rest goes elsewhere. Genesis 41:34-36 reads, *"Let Pharaoh do this, and let him appoint overseers over the land, and take up the fifth part of the land of Egypt's produce in the seven plenteous years. Let them gather all the food of these good years that come, and store grain under the hand of Pharaoh for food in the cities, and let them keep it. The food will be to supply the land against the seven years of famine, which will be in the land of Egypt; so that the land will not perish through the famine."* Joseph placed the farmers who were selling their land to prevent starvation on the 80/20 plan, under which Pharaoh received one-fifth of the harvest, and they lived off the remaining 80%. Many successful believers live off a variation of the 80/20 plan, where they save 10%, tithe 10%, and live off the remaining 80%. Living on 80% is a challenging concept for some and requires determination to achieve, but it is intended to help you. Many people think back to prosperous years with little worry, even as they drown in debt. That wasn't extra money you spent; it was emergency money that you would need. If you start earning more, save it, don't spend it.

HANDLING FINANCES LIKE A CEO

Stewards are like CEOs running a company for the corporate group, which in our case is God. They work and live off the budget. Proverbs 27:23 says, *"Know well the state of your flocks, and pay attention to your herds."* Budgeting reflects the values you prioritize. There are four key elements in creating a **BUDGET (Balance Unveils Debt, Giving Envisioned Tasks)**. First, you must calculate your expenses. Secondly, you should determine your income using a wage calculation. Next, you need to set your payoff and savings goals. Lastly, you should keep track of your expenses. You can only manage what you can measure. Laying out all your bills and expenses isn't tricky. Take a three-month look at your spending from your bank account statements and determine what was needed and what wasn't. Consider saving as an expense that comes off the top. Instead of having to categorize every single expense as essential or not, you take 20% of your paycheck and deposit half of it directly into your savings account, and use the other half for giving. The rest is yours to spend on bills and as you see fit.

Money is currency, and like the currents of the ocean, it goes out as quickly as it comes in. The CEO's primary responsibility is to generate revenue, enabling investors to maintain their standard of living. For the steward, those investors are your immediate family living in your household. We need to make sure we receive the proper education, skills, training, and mentorship (I said that word again, mentors) that will help us earn what we need. Think about the life you want to live and how much you would need to make to sustain that life. What kind of training do you need to make that sort of income eventually? Would that job align with your skills, gifts, and temperament? When you can answer all these questions, you have a 3 to 5-year plan for your financial life.

A key factor in generating income is leads and advertising. A lead is a potential customer who may be interested in the business or its services. These are the people that business reaches out to personally. Advertisements are displays that make a company or product attractive to the public. If you are employed, you are the product that needs to create leads by networking with those in related fields. There may be a company offering a better location, pay, and benefits that suit your plans. Advertise yourself by sharing how you can help a company meet its goals. Entry-level jobs don't require experience, so a good interview will suffice. Mid-level jobs may require you to refine your resume and hone your interview skills. High-level jobs will probably require a professional career portfolio. While others are turning in their resumes, your professional portfolio will stand out. A professional portfolio consists of a resume, performance evaluations, a sample of your writing, a list of special projects you were involved in, copies of degrees or educational certificates, certificates of awards, community service records, and recognition letters. Bind your portfolio with each topic in a labeled section, accompanied by a cover page that states your name. Being better prepared than the competition is a key factor in improving both your business and your personal life.

WAGE CALCULATION - 50¢ RULE

The second part is your wage calculation. If you're going to live life to its fullest, you have to know what you have coming in. It's essential to earn a sufficient income when planning your career or applying for a new job. That's where the 50¢ rule comes in. It is an estimate of how much **INCOME (Inflowing Net Cash Of Money Earned)** you can anticipate. The average full-time employee has a 40-hour workweek and 52 weeks in a year. Forty hours a week x 52 weeks equals 2080 work hours in a year. If you made $1 an hour, that would be $ 2,080 a year. Dividing by two means that for every $0.50 you earn in wages, you receive $1,040 in income per year, which is roughly just over $1,000 for every fifty cents earned. This figure, of course, does not include overtime. Therefore, a person earning $20 an hour can expect to earn just over $40,000 if they consistently work 40 hours a week. For greater accuracy, add $40 for every $0.50. Such as for a $20-an-hour wage (20 x 2) x $40 = $1,600. The individual making $20 an hour, with an actual income, would be $41,600 per year. This rule is convenient in estimating earnings when planning your personal finances.

SAVING LIKE A CEO

> Luke 14:28 For which of you, desiring to build a tower, doesn't first sit down and count the cost, to see if he has enough to complete it?

The third step is achieving your debt payoff and savings goals. CEOs are employees of the company and are paid first, alongside every other employee. Treating your savings like any other bill helps you live by the 80/20 rule. Some prefer to break the 80/20 rule down further into the 50-30-20 rule, where 50% of your spending allocates to essential needs, such as food, shelter, insurance, and transportation. On this plan, you spend 30% of your income on wants, such as clothes, restaurants, vacations, and entertainment, and the remaining 20% on savings. The individual would take the amount they give from the savings amount. However, the simplest form of budgeting is what I call the No-Think rule: you pay all your essential expenses and savings first, and simply live off the rest. To develop a savings habit, it is important to pay yourself first. You can automate this process, and in some cases, jobs offer split direct deposits: a certain amount of your paycheck is deposited into your checking account, and the rest into a savings account. From here, you will establish a rainy-day savings account, which financial planners generally recommend to be 3-6 months of your expenses. If you're going to make the most of what life has to offer, add a holiday and vacation savings account to finance your enjoyment. CEOs make sure they receive bonuses for all their hard work. Your bonus comes in the form of treating yourself to something small or large from time to time.

THE COLD SHOULDER OF DEBT

Years ago, I had a conversation with an enthusiastic young man in his 20s and asked him what he wanted to do with his life. He retorted, "I want to be a CEO." I said, 'That's simple: start a charity feeding the poor and incorporate it, and you will be a CEO.' He said, "Not like that." To him, CEO meant wealth rather than responsibility. I knew he was already in debt, and his skill and education level were those of a respectable blue-collar worker. So, I asked him, "Do you know what a descending dollar report is?" He said no. I said, "Why would people place you over their business when you don't know about business?" He has still never learned about business, so he never became a CEO. The descending dollar report is a review of money spent from the top to the bottom. The report identifies areas where you can trim costs by focusing on reducing the top three expenses in a quarter. The snowball method employs this approach to list debts from highest to lowest, but typically begins by paying off the smallest debt first.

If we are managing our finances like a CEO, we must understand the distinction between good debt and bad debt. Good debt is the purchase of assets that appreciate or gain value, such as real estate, stocks, bonds, or collectibles. These are things you can either leverage or sell for a higher price later. Bad debt is an asset whose value depreciates over time. Cars, jewelry, and equipment depreciate the moment they are purchased. Romans 13:8 says we should, *"Owe no one anything, except to love one another; for he who loves his neighbor has fulfilled the law."* It is crucial to get out of bad debt as soon as possible. The law of supply and demand determines value, and there is less demand for used goods. Some luxury brands, such as Cartier or Rolex watches, may appreciate due to high demand, but this generally doesn't occur with most watches or jewelry, and it definitely doesn't occur with automobiles or other items where wear and tear are a consideration. Not only do we have good and bad debt, but we also have reasonable debt. Reasonable debts are things that economists declare as bad debt, but you need. You may need a car for dependable transportation because the time it saves you is a commodity that cannot be recovered. Never feel bad about debts you can pay if there is a reasonable need.

If you have serious **DEBT (Doing Everything But Trusting)**, the most important thing is to stop creating new debt, which takes self-control and wisdom. Proverbs 22:7 says, *"The rich rule over the poor. The borrower is servant to the lender."* Debt is bondage, and it often means you are living beyond your means. If you have cut everything you can and are still short, then income is the problem, and you will need an additional source of income, such as a second job or a side hustle. I have seen people move back in with their parents to lower their costs and pay off debts, but since they don't change their spending habits, they end up staying much longer than anticipated. Hopefully, you have some emergency savings; if not, consider using half of what you should have saved and paying extra on the debt with the lowest balance first —a method known as the snowball approach. For example, if you have debts of $ 4,000, $ 6,000, $12,000, and $20,000, you would make the regular payments on each **LOAN (Lending Offered Accommodates Need)**, but you would apply all extra money for repayment to the lowest loan. Once completed, you place the premium, plus the extra money you were paying, on the next loan, paying each off in turn. The rationale for starting with the lowest is to gain a quick victory and motivation as you see one debt wiped out. It's like a snowball rolling in the snow that gets bigger and picks up momentum as it goes.

While snowballing is the most effective method due to the motivation and emotional reward of achieving a quick victory, the avalanche method is more efficient. You are paying a higher amount in interest on the highest debt, so the smart thing is to start with the highest and work your way down. Both the snowball and avalanche methods require that you live below your means and not go back to spending once you have paid off a debt or two. The avalanche method takes the same approach, but starts with the largest sum. After paying it off, the extra funds are applied to the next loan. It takes much longer to pay off the first loan, so there is no quick motivational boost. Those who are very disciplined may prefer to pay off the debts with the highest interest rates or the most considerable debts first. However, disciplined spenders rarely end up in debt.

CUTTING COSTS LIKE A BUSINESS

The fourth thing we need to do is watch our expenses. A general rule of thumb is that if businesses do something to earn or save money, you should be doing it too. They look for vendors who provide the best goods at the most reasonable prices. For you, this may mean clipping coupons in your spare time or purchasing produce from one store and canned goods from another. Businesses often purchase in bulk to save money, so having a shopping buddy with whom you buy in bulk and split the products can be beneficial. During the holiday season, you can find large household items on sale. Instead of purchasing a new car for the upcoming year, you may be able to get a better deal on the current year's stock and take advantage of the end-of-year sale when dealers are clearing their inventory. A certified pre-owned car would offer you an even better deal, saving you thousands and allowing you to pay off the note sooner. Some of us are financially wounded but haven't stopped the bleeding. Haggai 1:6 says, "*You have sown much, and bring in little. You eat, but you don't have enough. You drink, but you aren't filled with drink. You clothe yourselves, but no one is warm; and he who earns wages earns wages to put them into a bag with holes in it.*" Sewing up your budget involves eliminating unnecessary expenses, such as bank fees, that consume your income. If you have a balance on a high-interest credit card, consider transferring it to a card with a lower interest rate. Consider limiting eating out to special occasions only and being mindful of your spending.

Most of the things we thought we had to have end up being thrown away or traded in within 3 to 5 years. Buy things that last, and spend only on what you need. Businesses have maintenance personnel who repair items within their scope and oversee vendor services for tasks outside their expertise. Most maintenance crews are required to submit three bids before hiring a vendor to work on the electrical, plumbing, or other areas. Try to fix what you can, and don't just hire the first person because you have a need. Some people will charge you more when they think you are too anxious to complete it. Limit your wants to the essentials. It isn't wise to spend money just because you have it. I like to inventory groceries, toiletries, and household items, just like the stores do, so that I can purchase them in bulk at a lower price.

Another aspect of cutting costs, as businesses do, is avoiding emotional spending, impulse shopping, and fads. If you feel depressed, only take a little cash with you when you shop, intentionally leaving the cards at home. Stick to your list, and a good rule is to never grocery shop while you are hungry. It will cause you to **BUY (Bargains Unleash Yearning)** junk food you don't need. Cheap products can be of poor quality, and while expensive products are usually superior, you are paying extra for the name. If you have to choose, opt for the middle lane where you can get good quality and reasonable prices. Not only is the middle reasonable, but it also helps you save time on decision-making, since what you do is generally already determined.

TAX ADVANTAGES

The CEO generates revenue for the company by identifying the most effective tax breaks and tax shelters to apply for. We call these tax advantages. One of the biggest complaints about companies is that they often fail to pay their fair share of taxes. Some states offer lower taxes to attract new consumers and businesses, thereby boosting their economies. They legally receive tax breaks and shelters in exchange for creating jobs and businesses that boost our economy. The new jobs not only grow GDP, but they also provide a base of new employees to tax. So instead of taxing the company, they tax us. Our charitable donations are tax-deductible, but I have heard some say they don't deduct them from their taxes because they were gifts to God. Well, deducting it and getting money in return allows for greater giving or investment. Consumers use tax returns to purchase more things they don't really need. CEOs use their tax shelters to pay off debts and invest in further growth.

Up to 90% of small businesses overpay their taxes by failing to keep accurate records and receipts. Well, you are probably part of the 90% of people who do too. Your side hustle also generates business, grows the GDP, and allows you to apply for tax shelters and write-offs that you could not have otherwise. You may be able to write off office space rented by you in your own home, as well as a percentage of your car note, cell phone bill, and internet services used for business purposes, and meals where you discuss your business. Tax breaks are an eligibility you apply for. These require you to itemize and keep receipts, but lead to greater returns. Consider using the extra cash for your return either to pay off debt or invest. If you tried it, you know it works. If you receive an extra $ 2,000 each year on your tax return after ten years, you could have an additional $20,000 invested, earning money from **TRIED (Trade, Returns, Interest, Earnings, Dividends).** As stewards of God, we must be honest: starting a side business that you plan to break even on or lose money on, in order to gain a greater tax return, is unethical. However, if companies are taking advantage of tax breaks by generating new businesses, so should you.

SHOPPING AT SLOT MACHINES

If you have ever been to a casino, the slot machines are up front. They are visually appealing, taking up the most floor space because they generate the most revenue for the casino. The games you have the best chance of winning, such as blackjack, are at the back. Stores also put their most profitable items and best sellers up front, but if you go just a little farther down the aisle, you will find the products that are the best deal for you. Remember, they are selling a name, but you are there to purchase a product, not a name. The only time I recommend buying a name is if you have invested in the company. I want to spend where I have stock. If you have investments in the company, it's beneficial to purchase their products and encourage others to do the same within reason.

The second area of slot machine shopping is subscription services that give you the experience you want but waste your money. Subscription services began in the 1800s with milk deliveries and gradually expanded to include magazines and other products. Refrigeration didn't become common until the 1920s, so milk deliveries were very regular. Many families wasted milk by not using it all before the next delivery. Today, some companies exist solely as subscription services, mainly focusing on products, entertainment, or experiences. The consulting firm West Monroe found that the average U.S. household pays $237 per month for subscription services, many of which are likely to go unused. Pay for services that you use, not those that you think you may need. Gym memberships are beneficial if you're showing up regularly, but if you only go occasionally, consider canceling the service and start exercising outside. If you want to spend less, consider cutting back on a few subscriptions and pulling the curtains back so you can turn off the lights.

THE RULE OF 72

Savings, just like investments, take time to grow. Proverbs 13:11 says, *"Dishonest money dwindles away, but whoever gathers money little by little makes it grow (NIV)."* Saving a little money regularly can lead to significant wealth. Understand that time and interest can make a little go a long way. **RULES (Restrictions Utilizing Limits Engaging Standards)** are to help you. The rule of 72, which governs interest, basically says that if you take an annual interest rate and divide it into 72, the answer you get tells you how many years it would take to double your money. If you deposited $5,000 at an 8% interest rate, then after 9 years (72 divided by 8 equals 9), you would have approximately $10,000. At a 6% interest rate, $5,000 would take 12 years for your savings or investment to earn the additional $5,000 to double your money. The Rule of 72 is a rule of thumb that approximates the effect of compound interest.

EARNING INTEREST ABOVE INFLATION

Inflation is a loss of purchasing power as prices for goods and services rise. The escalation often occurs when a nation decides to increase its money supply by printing more than usual. Remember that a monetary value derives from societal acceptance, and if vendors widely no longer accept $10 for what is now $12, that is inflation. These affect both the consumer price index and the wholesale price index. A currency loses value when prices rise, allowing it to buy fewer goods and services. This loss of purchasing power impacts the general cost of living. Inflation requires savings and investments to earn interest, as the same amount of money would be worth less in the future. The interest you earn needs to outpace inflation, or what you have saved or invested will be worth less. The COVID-19 pandemic led to a 7% surge in US and global inflation, triggering a recession as gross domestic product (GDP) declined. A recession causes a rise in interest rates to keep pace. We must maximize the interest we earn so the money we have doesn't buy less than it could.

An inflation penalty occurs when workers receive an annual raise that is lower than the rate of inflation. If you receive a 2% raise and the inflation rate is 4%, your income has less purchasing power than it did previously. Working where you are valued is essential. Businesses often recommend that you not discuss your pay rate with coworkers, but it is illegal for them to deny you the ability to do so. Loyal workers often receive low increases, while new employees receive premium pay for the same role. The most loyal employees are often the most overworked and sometimes underpaid. It is not personal, it's just business. Companies are in the habit of saving wherever they can. Shopping around to secure a better deal isn't disloyalty; it is being loyal to yourself first. Many people are losing thousands of dollars a year in financial stability simply because companies that raise prices due to inflation don't pay their employees at the same rate.

RETIREMENT SAVING PLANS

Your CEO has the best retirement package that money can buy. The three primary retirement savings plans are pensions, 401(k), and IRAs. Pensions are employer-guaranteed plans in which monthly benefits are paid based on salary and years of service. The money comes from employers, but they also allow employees to contribute to increase payouts. A 401(k) is a payroll deduction plan, normally pretax, offered by employers, in which contributions are automatically deducted from the employee's paycheck in an amount they decide. Some employers decide to contribute in a way similar to a pension plan, but this is becoming rarer. An Individual Retirement Account (IRA) is a personal retirement account funded solely by the individual. IRAs offer a wider range of investment options but have contribution limits. Traditional IRAs offer tax-deductible contributions, while Roth IRAs use after-tax dollars and grow tax-free, with tax-free payouts upon retirement.

Retirees need to stay busy, so the community organizations and help programs you become involved with while working become even more critical when retiring. When it comes to retirement, it's not how much income you have, but what you do with it. Those who start and continue making small contributions in their 20s and 30s will typically have well-funded retirements. The later you start, the more you will need to contribute monthly to have a comfortable retirement. However, many people have little or no retirement savings. They have to work longer, depend on children, or go without things because they can't afford them in retirement. Many end up depending on government-funded programs like Social Security, which provides a monthly benefit to qualifying disabled individuals, retirees who have paid into the system, and their loved ones. Regardless of where you are with your retirement savings, the most important thing is to fix your budget so you are contributing what you will need for retirement.

LIVING MORE WITH LESS

There is a story of two lumberjacks competing in a wood-cutting contest. The younger person works tirelessly, cutting down trees nonstop. The older logger takes breaks. At the end of the day, the older logger has cut down more trees than the younger one. The younger exclaims, "How did you beat me? I cut down trees nonstop, and I saw you take breaks." The older logger replied, "I rested to gain strength and resharpen my ax. Look at your axe; it is dull and not well-maintained. I took care of my tool, and it took care of me."

For years, we have heard people say, "Work smarter, not harder." Indeed, enjoying life is also about not just what you have, but how smartly you prepare. Like the wise lumberjack, we need to start by taking breaks to rest and sharpen our tools. Well, steward, that tool is yourself. There is a reason God instituted the Sabbath. The sabbath is a day of rest to replenish you physically, mentally, spiritually, and emotionally. Jesus is speaking in Mark 2:27, and says, *"He said to them, The Sabbath was made for man, not man for the Sabbath."* The rest God gave is for our benefit. Taking time each week to spend with God and family, and slowing down to refresh and enjoy life, will de-stress your days. Too many of us are either like the younger lumberjack working nonstop, taking up a lot of our time but not making as significant an impact as we think, or like the unnamed spectator who lies back and watches the event. We should work smart and play smarter.

DESIGN ON A DIME

My wife doesn't really watch television. The only shows you will catch her watching are Christian TV or home-and-garden shows. The first show she forced me to watch (I mean, she had me watch with her) was "Design on a Dime." The show would copy the look of an expensively designed space and, for just around $1,000, innovatively recreate the room. It was do-it-yourself heaven. You could get what you want while saving money. Enjoying life is the same. You can spend a lot and have numerous experiences to remember, or you can be innovative and repeat the same type of experiences, deriving the same level of enjoyment from your life. Joy doesn't come from what you accumulate but from what you appreciate, so living more with less begins in the heart. The condition of our hearts will determine the level of peace, joy, and fulfillment we experience. Living more with less means focusing on the critical things in your life, decluttering the mess, and making your life a priority.

THE 24 HOUR RULE

The simplest way to declutter your life is to get rid of what you don't use or wear, and then use the 24-hour rule before making new purchases. Give yourself 24 hours to regulate your emotions before making purchases or life decisions. The extra day gives you time to decide whether it's something you really need or just something you wanted for the moment. Waiting 24 hours leads to better decision-making and greater financial discipline. Proverbs 19:11 says, *"A person's wisdom yields patience; it is to one's glory to overlook an offense (NIV)."* A common characteristic of wise people is that they are willing to **WAIT (Wisdom Always Involves Time)**. Patience is the wise mind we then take into our activities. We can't wait until retirement to get active; our enjoyment of life should start now. A steward lives in service, but that doesn't mean that God doesn't want happy people in His house. If you have money, spend it wisely without wasting it. If money is an issue, decide what you like and try to do it on a dime. My goal is to visit all 50 states with my wife, then the US territories, and I seek to do so when flights and hotels are cheap. I know a doctor who loves camping and seeks to visit every national park in the US. Having vacation goals helps you to budget for what you will do. I mention some of these types of things in my book, "200 Tips for a Successful Marriage," which may be helpful for budgeting while still having fun. Here are some of the tips condensed.

- Use 3-day weekends as short getaways. You only have to travel far enough away to feel unfamiliar. If you have no money, consider doing a weekend house swap with a friend. So, two families enjoy the change of pace.
- A dating system that alternates between familiar places, new places, borrowed items to save costs, and locations that promote short travel.
- Attend free public events and fairs within the limited budget you have allocated.

- Watch professional or semi-professional plays performed at community and college theater shows.
- If you love sports but don't want to pay the high pro price, consider supporting a semi-pro team. You will have the same atmosphere at a smaller venue for a lower price.
- A Forget Me Not Calendar doing small extraordinary things weekly for the one you love. Purchase cards and small gifts monthly, then hide them and give them a gift a week.
- Share discount codes between friends for vacation, theme parks, and events. Expand your network, expand your opportunities.

A life lived today is not regretted tomorrow. Ultimately, doing more with less comes down to what you value and investing in your own joy. It's all the little moments that add up to a big life. The steward who prepares for the future safely still has to live in the present. Life is like taking a long trip with ups and downs, so we should enjoy the journey as we travel the road.

FINANCIAL TERMS ABC'S

· · · · ·

Annuities - insurance contracts paid out to retirees concerned about outliving their savings.

Balance - a financial statement providing a snapshot of assets, liabilities, and shareholder equity

Capital - money or assets used to generate returns

Debt Ratio - a metric measuring leverage by comparing its debt to assets

Equity - the remaining value of an asset after paying any debt owed

Futures – agreement to buy or sell assets at a set date and price

Gross Domestic Product (GDP) scorecard of government health based on consumer & government spending, exports, and investments.

Hedge Fund – a private pool of money managed by professionals

Indemnity - a contractual agreement in insurance policies to prevent damage or loss.

Junk bonds - high-yield, high-risk bonds from a company with a lower credit rating

Kickback - illegal payment for preferential treatment or service

Leverage - taking on debt to increase future returns from a product or investment

Mutual Fund - money from investors to purchase a diversified portfolio of securities

Net worth - the monetary value of the assets after subtracting the value of liabilities.

Outsourcing - hiring external parties to perform tasks cheaper than in-house efforts

Profit & Loss Statement - snapshot of a company's profitability, for a quarter or year

Qualified Dividend – payment made to stock owner taxed at capital gains tax rates.

Return on Investment - a financial ratio measuring profit generated relative to its cost

Securities - investment contracts sold by corporations and governments to raise capital.

Trust - an estate planning tool holding assets for individuals for financial protection

Unsecured Loan – a loan based on creditworthiness instead of collateral

Venture Capital - private equity financing for startup companies and small businesses

Wealth Management - investment advisory services for affluent clients

Xenocurrency - currency traded in markets outside of domestic borders

Yields - the amount of money in interest or dividends that stock investors receive

Zombie Debt - old or not legally collectable debts that debt collectors still attempt to collect.

Scan to watch video: The Boss Principle

CHAPTER TEN

BUSINESS FOR THE GLORY OF GOD

. . . .

2 SAMUEL 22:25-28

Therefore Yahweh has rewarded me according to my righteousness, According to my cleanness in his eyesight. With the merciful you will show yourself merciful. With the perfect man you will show yourself perfect. With the pure you will show yourself pure. With the crooked you will show yourself shrewd. You will save the afflicted people, but your eyes are on the arrogant, that you may bring them down..

S tewardship is a responsibility. God appoints His steward over His belongings and expects the steward to manage His goods faithfully. 2 Samuel 22:21 says, *"Yahweh rewarded me according to my righteousness. He rewarded me according to the cleanness of my hands."* While we know all of our righteousness is as filthy rags (Isaiah 64:6), there is nothing we can do to earn salvation. In this case, the Bible speaks to the righteous cause of the individual, how God blessed King David on earth by providing for him and protecting him. When David's motives and cause aligned with God, he performed his work with clean hands. David was committed to God's **GLORY (Gracious Lauding Of Righteous Yearning)**. The blessings and rewards in stewardship are determined not only by God's faithfulness but also by ours. God rewards the steward according to four characteristic traits. These four traits relate to our reliability, conduct, wisdom, and motives in our stewardship.

RELIABILITY

You can only rely on what is faithful. Those things that won't fail you when the chips are down. Faithfulness involves the steward's consistent behavior in managing God's resources. Persistence may help you acquire things, but consistency is what keeps what you have gained. God showing Himself faithful to the faithful means that God rewards faithfulness by being even more faithful. Matthew 25:21 reads. *"His lord said to him, 'Well done, good and faithful servant. You have been faithful over a few things, I will set you over many things. Enter into the joy of your lord."* As the steward consistently does their best to manage Our Heavenly Father's goods, God is faithful to provide for the steward and their household. Faithfulness gives God something to bless and gives people someone to trust. Faithfulness requires consistent effort and builds upon it, gaining trust, security, and loyalty. If you're selling products or services, this will help keep your customers.

GODLY IN CONDUCT

Our conduct opens or closes doors. People prefer pleasant exchanges, not conflict. That's why businesses spend billions every year on customer service etiquette and management. As stewards of God, we represent Him as we conduct our business. Titus 1:7 says, *"For the overseer must be blameless, as God's steward, not self-pleasing, not easily angered, not given to wine, not violent, not greedy for dishonest gain.*" Although Paul applied this concept to ministry, the same principle applies to life; the conduct of those who oversee matters is essential. Blameless means that the steward keeps their integrity in all their dealing. God wants His stewards to behave as He would in His own business dealings. I heard someone say that they won't hire a manager who cheats on their spouse, because if the person you sleep with can't trust you, neither can they. A steward should never cheat or take advantage of anyone. Godly conduct gives God a good representation wherever you go. We are the image of the one we represent. Whether that is God, a brand, or a company we work for. People see what we represent through our conduct, and giving a bad impression of a good thing is harmful.

People can see when a fish is out of water. They flap around and appear to be very active, but are dying inside. That's what it's like to have impure motives. You can only fool people for so long, especially when they have discernment coming from eyes that see and ears that hear. Purity speaks to our motives. When we handle the possessions, the Lord has put in our hands, are we doing it with a right heart? Titus 1:15 says, *"To the pure, all things are pure, but to those who are defiled and unbelieving, nothing is pure; but both their mind and their conscience are defiled."* If your motives are not right, you are not right. You may have the right answer, but with the wrong heart, it means little. A heart of greed, envy, or selfishness will prevent the steward from receiving the blessings that God has ordained for them.

FAITHFUL AND WISE

As we have said repeatedly, the Steward is a manager of God's goods. Alongside faithfulness, another essential characteristic is the application of **WISDOM (Witty Insights Shows Discernment Opening Minds)**. Luke 12:42-43 reads, *"The Lord said, 'Who then is the faithful and wise steward, whom his lord will set over his household, to give them their portion of food at the right times? Blessed is that servant whom his lord will find doing* so when he comes". The steward who operates across these multiple veins of good character will succeed. I know we just mentioned faithfulness, but it is so essential that we need to go deeper. So important that many have lost out on the blessing God would have given them if they had remained committed to Him. Faithfulness is summed up in *Luke 16:10, "He who is faithful in a very little is faithful also in much. He who is dishonest in a very little is also dishonest."* We have already discussed faithful giving, but there are a few additional areas of faithfulness that need consideration.

CREDIT

> *Proverbs 16:8 Better a little with righteousness than much gain with injustice.*

In my early twenties, I purchased my first few cars from the Long Beach auction. They were **CHEAP (Cost Has Everyone Appreciating Price)**, and a few were dependable, but some were not. Eventually, I went to a car lot to purchase a car, and they offered me an 18% interest rate. I told the man at the counter that I don't have bad credit because I have always paid cash for everything. He said, "You don't have bad credit history, you have no credit history, and that is bad credit." I wrongly thought that just paying cash meant I wouldn't mess up my credit, but you can't have what you never established. When you live in a capitalist society, they measure faithfulness by your credit score. The faithful steward will be successful in their endeavors. Your credit report is a record of how you have paid your bills and managed money over time. The more consistently you make your bill payments, the higher your credit score. The credit score associated with your credit report is a valuation of the steward's name. Credit scores can range from 300 to 900, with most people falling within the 600-700 range.

Credit doesn't depend on what you make; instead, your credit score derives from what creditors can verify about you, such as your payment history, credit utilization, age of credit, credit mix, and the number of inquiries on your report. Several factors determine your credit score, including whether you pay your bills on time and how you manage the credit you already have. It is essential to pay your bills on time to increase your credit score. A high credit score will allow you to receive lower interest rates when you buy a house, a car, or apply for a business loan. It is equally important not to be maxed out on your credit cards. Lenders are looking to see how you steward the money God has given you.

Remember Proverbs 22:1 says that, *"A good name is more desirable than great riches, and loving favor is better than silver and gold."* Your Credit score is a valuation of what lenders think your name represents. By maintaining a good relationship with your creditors, you will increase your value more than you would otherwise. A good credit history helps us to prepare for our destiny. Ecclesiastes 7:1 says, *"A good name is better than fine perfume; and the day of death better than the day of one's birth."* Many people were born into poverty, but by stewarding their resources correctly, they were able to improve their situation. They worked hard and improved their social and financial standings. Many took it upon themselves to do better socially and financially than their parents and encouraged their children to do the same. Remember, it is never too late to build. That's why Proverbs 3:3 tells us never to let love and faithfulness leave us. By living a life of love and faithfulness, you can rebuild your credit. If people believe you will repay them, they will lend you what you need.

PIGGYBACKING ON CREDIT

The best thing I could have done when they offered me an 18% interest rate to buy a car would have been to wait and fix my credit before purchasing. Paying bills on time is one of the most effective ways to improve your credit score. Since derogatory items remain on your credit report for seven years, it can take time. Automating your bill payment is a good method. Using Esperian Boost, a free service that links your bank account and allows the inclusion of rent, utilities, streaming services, and phone bills on your credit report, can increase your credit score. Good credit utilization is using 30% or less of available credit on credit cards. We should obtain a free credit report to review and dispute any discrepancies that we believe are incorrect or fraudulent. Disputing charges will temporarily remove the derogatory report; if the charges are found valid, they will remain on your report. If there are collections on your report, agree to settle them. Sometimes, you can receive a discount and request that the collection agency stop reporting the derogatory mark once the debt is paid in full.

There are no true quick fixes, as the goal isn't just to achieve an average credit score, but a good one. The simplest method to increase your credit score quickly is the credit **PIGGYBACK (Person Interested Giving Generosity Yields Benefit Allowing Credit Kickback)**. Piggybacking is when someone with an excellent credit history adds you as an authorized user on their credit card. Authorized users are not responsible for the card's debt, as they are not joint account holders. As an authorized user, you receive all of the credit history associated with that card, including the age of the account, payment history, and utilization rate. You have no risk of having to pay, and the individual you are piggybacking on their credit doesn't have to provide you with a card or card number, so there is no risk to them of you making a purchase. It's a win for you and a kindness for them. You can instantly receive years of credit history because of the kindness of a family member or close friend willing to help.

CO-SIGNING

Co-signing is a way for individuals with poor credit to build their credit scores by leveraging those with good **CREDIT (Confidence Related Earns Double In Trials)**. A lender may request a cosigner when a borrower has a poor credit history. The lender is asking the co-signer to assume responsibility if the borrower defaults on the loan. If someone asks you to cosign for them, the first thing you must consider is that the person asking usually does not have a good habit of paying their bills on time. If the borrower defaults on the loan, the cosigner is responsible for making the monthly payments until the borrower repays the loan. The cosigner should also be aware of what the Bible says about cosigning.

The first thing to mention is that co-signing is not wise. Proverbs 17:18 says, *"A man void of understanding strikes hands, and becomes collateral in the presence of his neighbor."* Often, people find themselves in financial trouble because they are living beyond their means. People who can only afford a used car will try to get you to cosign for a new car they want but can only afford if something doesn't interrupt their income. When unexpected financial problems arise, they default on the loan. This means the **LOSS (Losing Our Shirt Stupid)** is yours. Proverbs 27:13 says, *"Take his garment when he puts up collateral for a stranger. Hold it for a wayward woman!"* Some people, including family members, may use your emotions to persuade you to cosign a loan. They are usually very genuine about their appreciation for cosigning, but later, their genuineness can turn to a nonchalant attitude, as if the bill is not their concern.

COLLATERAL

> Proverbs 22:26-27, Don't you be one of those who strike hands, of those who are collateral for debts. If you don't have means to pay, why should he take away your bed from under you?

Collateral is a property that guarantees a loan and demonstrates a borrower's commitment to the lender. Putting up collateral is not a bad thing in itself, but it is when you can't pay. Putting up property that you can't afford to redeem is not a very smart move. Many people have lost their homes by putting their property up as collateral for bail for a loved one. Only to have that loved one skip town, leaving them stuck with a massive bill. When you put something up as collateral, you should be aware that you may lose it. Placing property as **COLLATERAL (Creditors Offer Loose Lending Alternative That Encourages Risking Asset Loss)** can lead to forced seizure, in which a judicial sale or a court order to sell the property is issued to pay off a debt.

PARETO PRINCIPLE - 80/20 RULE

Another iteration of the 80/20 rule comes from economist Vilfredo Pareto, who noticed that people naturally divide into the vital few. He discovered that most economic activity follows the principle that 80% of a company's income comes from approximately 20% of its customers, and that 80% of referrals come from 20% of its referral sources. The principle helps us prioritize tasks, focusing on the 20% that yields the most from our time and effort.

Investing

> *Proverbs 17:16 Why is there money in the hand of a fool to buy wisdom, since he has no understanding?*

In Matthew 25:14-29, Jesus told us a parable about three stewards. The master left and expected them to all **INVEST (Initiating New Ventures Earned Some Talents)** his talents, which were a form of money. The master didn't care whether it was starting a business or opening an interest-earning bank account. He just wanted them to build income. The unfaithful steward suffered from investment procrastination. The best time to plant a tree is 20 years ago. If we didn't do it, then we should start now. Investing $250 per month starting at age 25 will yield $878,820.30 at age 65, assuming an annual return of 8%. If you start at 35, the same strategy would net you $342,365.30. That's a difference of $536,455.00 that you would not have earned. Before you think that earning 8% a year is unrealistic, note that the S&P 500 and Nasdaq both average over 10% every year. At this rate, investing just $50 every month in an account from the time a child is born will yield over $700,000 by the time they reach 50.

Investing, when done correctly, can build income for you and your family. I have seen people claiming they have no money to invest, but they play the lottery and never win. The fact that low-income households spend four times as much on the lottery as high-income households reveals a significant disparity. Their chance of making money investing is much greater than their chance of winning the lottery. There are four principles that we should adhere to when investing. The first is not just to rush in. Emotions lead to a financial train wreck. Proverbs 21:5 says, *'The plans of the diligent surely lead to profit; and everyone who is hasty surely rushes to poverty.'* You are investing in healthy people, companies, and products, not sales pitches or fads. Financial planners can help, but you should check whether the individual has any complaints filed against them. Even if they are a bit too showy about their personal wealth to get you on board with their program, it can be a clue that it's a scam or a pyramid scheme. Check the company's ratings and the average return on investment it provides for its clients. If a new product interests you, learn about its market demand before investing in its development. Hesitancy leads to the second principle, learning. Proverbs 24:3-4 says, *"Through wisdom a house is built; by understanding it is established; by knowledge the rooms are filled with all rare and beautiful treasure."* As the saying goes, "Knowledge is knowing a tomato is a fruit, wisdom is not putting it in a fruit salad." Studying will give you knowledge. Most people who invest haven't taken two hours to learn how to read a financial index that tracks their investments' performance. People who don't occasionally check their investments may find themselves involved with unscrupulous individuals who are counting on it. Knowledge becomes wisdom when used effectively. Wisdom doesn't come from studying; it comes from observing. Observe people, company values, and trends to make informed choices. Wisdom is not a guarantee that things outside your control will work out as you think. But if you make the best choices for yourself, then you can live with the outcome.

The third principle to remember about investing is waiting. Things take time to grow, and withdrawing from an investment in a healthy company or commodity can be costly. Job 6:11 asks the question, *"What strength do I have, that I should still hope? What prospects, that I should be patient? (NIV)?"* If the company is strong but the stock is weak, you should probably invest more, expecting a rebound in the stock price. There are three things that, although they decline, always snap back stronger: they are gross domestic product, the stock market, and property values. The S&P 500 has consistently delivered strong returns, and most of us haven't invested in it. In all our endeavors, it is essential first to gain an understanding (Proverbs 4:7). Wealth accumulation happens slowly, and even if you have a great job or business, good planning can lead to HENRY's (High Earning, **Not Rich Yet Syndrome).** Henry's is where your income is high, but your plan to pay off school debt and invest for the future causes you to live frugally. Mentally, they know they are doing well, but it doesn't feel that way.

Ultimately, we don't want to put all our eggs in one basket. Ecclesiastes 11:2 says, *"Give a portion to seven, yes, even to eight; for you don't know what evil will be on the earth."* Diversifying your investments is a good way to secure them. It helps keep you from losing everything betting on the wrong horse. Diversifying your investments across multiple stocks, mutual funds, or other assets can help protect your portfolio. Using educated investing doesn't control the outcome. Though savings are insured, investments are not. Diversifying is assurance without insurance. You can be assured you won't lose everything, because all investments would have to fall in value simultaneously for that to happen. Even those who haven't saved enough to invest outside of their 401(k) or pension can **DIVERSIFY (Divide Investments Values Effectively Reduces Shortened Income From Yielding) by** getting multiple streams of income. Having a job, a side hustle, and a pension plan means you already have three streams of income. Some are large and some are small, but all lead to an increase.

Business Smarts

> *Proverbs 30:8-9 Remove far from me falsehood and lies. Give me neither poverty nor riches. Feed me with the food that is needful for me, lest I be full, deny you, and say, 'Who is Yahweh?' or lest I be poor, and steal, and so dishonor the name of my God.*

Financial literacy is a process. It includes learning how money works, tax strategies, investment principles, business fundamentals, professional skills, and personal discipline. Using them rightly is what brings glory to God. Whether you are investing or starting your own business, you need to be wise. The crowd you hang around will either make you or break you. The more you experience the Lord's hand of blessing, the fewer people you will have attached to you. For those who aren't on their way up, the new ways you talk and things you do will seem like a foreign language to them. And they are right, most people don't speak the language of gaining favor by doing what pleases God. God's way brings blessing, but is also a burden we bear. When conducting business for the glory of God, we must remember never to become greedy. Hebrews 13:5 says, *"Be free from the love of money, content with such things as you have, for he has said, I will in no way leave you, neither will I in any way forsake you."* When greed occurs, you no longer have possessions; your possessions have you. The purpose of a resource is to utilize it for a specific end. Greed makes the resource the end itself. Contentment shows God that His presence means more than our possessions.

God is a creator, and He placed humanity in charge of the resources of His creation. The way we handle those resources honors God, and our resourcefulness in business reflects His glory. Proverbs 18:16 tells us, *"A man's gift makes room for him, and brings him before great men."* We should continue to utilize all our abilities to innovate, specialize, or personalize our approach. Even if a million people are doing the same thing, our unique thumbprint should still have an impact on our sphere of influence. Doing business with God as the center of our life is hard work. There are corners that we can't cut. Proverbs 20:13 reads, *"Don't love sleep, lest you come to poverty. Open your eyes, and you shall be satisfied with bread."*

Living in the Los Angeles area, I recognize the late great Kobe Bryant, a member of the Lakers basketball franchise, was an integral part of the city's history and the Lakers' glory. He was a top player in the NBA, known for being the first to arrive at practice and the last to leave. He was great not only because of his talent, but also because he put in the effort others were unlikely to. He was not satisfied with a good performance; he sought an outstanding one every time. In one of his retirement interviews, an interviewer asked him what he would do now that he has retired. He responded that he would still get up early and hit the gym. He did what others were unwilling to do, even for themselves. It's that winning attitude, coupled with his skills and practice, that made him a champion. Remember that the only one you have to compete against is yourself. Other people are not the measure of your success. You are to be faithful in maximizing your abilities, and don't worry about what others do. We should strive to be outstanding, outperforming our last efforts and bringing glory to our God.

There is a difference between shopping as a vendor and shopping as a consumer. A vendor acts as a wholesaler, buying in bulk and bargaining for a better deal, and doesn't act as if they are the end goal of the product. Consumers are the retail or final end customers who will use or consume the product directly. Proverbs 20:14 reads, *"It's no good, it's no good,"* says *the buyer; but when he is gone his way, then he boasts."* Often, we shop as consumers, not vendors. We visit large retail stores that buy in bulk but sell items separately at a set price, which employees cannot negotiate. When I visited Cancun, Mexico, the hotel informed me that people generally expect to haggle over prices, so everything has a 30% markup over the actual value. When you purchase based on the listed price, vendors love it. Identify areas where you have leeway and consider speaking with those who may be able to offer you a better deal. You are not just a consumer; you are a kingdom shopper.

Whatever the steward does, they do as a representation of God. Proverbs 23:4-5 instructs us, *"Don't weary yourself to be rich. In your wisdom, show restraint. Why do you set your eyes on that which is not? For it certainly sprouts wings like an eagle and flies in the sky."* One of the first reality TV shows was "Lifestyles of the Rich and Famous," with Robin Leach. It was groundbreaking in its time, but soon replaced by the myriad of eye-popping modern shows designed to keep our attention. Keeping our eye on wealth is the way of the world. As stewards, our focus is on God and how to bring Him glory through our works of love and worship. We work from a sense of faithfulness and according to our purpose, driven by the outcome, not by income. That is our goal as stewards: to bring God glory.

TIED TO THE WRONG PEOPLE

• • • • •

2 Corinthians 6:14-15 Don't be unequally yoked with unbelievers, for what fellowship do righteousness and iniquity have? Or what fellowship does light have with darkness? What agreement does Christ have with Belial? Or what portion does a believer have with an unbeliever?

Did you know the words marriage or married never appear in the book of 2nd Corinthians? Yet when we say, don't be unequally yoked we usually interpret it as a restriction of being married to an unbeliever. It's a reference to Deuteronomy 22:10, which prohibits yoking a bull and a donkey together. The bull is stronger, and if plowing with a donkey, it would pull the donkey along. Donkeys are steadier and can plow on uneven land, such as hills, but they won't get much done when the stubborn ox won't move. The verse isn't about marriage but about establishing contracts and business agreements with unbelievers.

The unbeliever may seem strong, but you are steady. As stewards, we glorify God in our business dealings, and an unbeliever cannot do that. Certain practices and habits that impact you don't affect them. You will find yourself hee-hawing in complaint to an ox who doesn't listen. God dwells in and will lead you, not them. Contracts and yoking for work with those with whom you fundamentally disagree on their practices will lead to a future break that will hurt your investment. To glorify God, we must keep untainted, and the Lord will receive us (V. 17).

Scan to watch video: The Learning Principle

LIST OF ACRONYMS

Alms

Arrow

Bless

Bow

Budget

Bullet

Buy

Cheap

Collateral

Communion

Covenant

Credit

Cross

Debt

Demand

Diversify

Duty

Fact

Faith

Finances

First

Generous

Gift

Glory

Goal

Greed

Gun

Harvest

Hearts

Henry's

Honor

Income

Invest

Law

Led

Levite

Loan

Loss

Lucky

Mistake

Money

Move

Offering

Pies

Piggyback

Plan

Pots

Poverty

Product

Reap

Reaper

Redeem

Rules

Sacrifice

Sat

Save

Savings

Season

Seed

Service

Share

Sin

Steward

Stock

Supply

Tac

Tags

Tanstaafl

Test

Tis

Tithe

Tried

Trust

Wait

Wisdom